Cooking School
PROVENCE

Cooking School
PROVENCE

Shop, cook, and eat like a local

GUI GEDDA AND MARIE-PIERRE MOINE

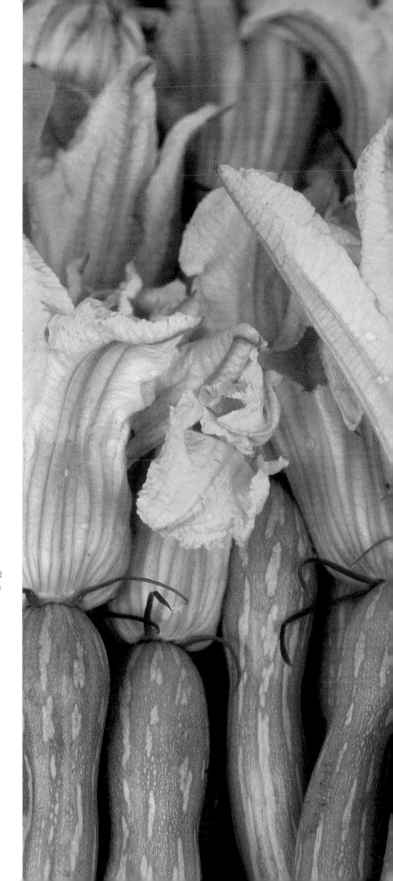

LONDON, NEW YORK, MELBOURNE, MUNICH, AND DELHI

Project Manager and Editor	Norma MacMillan
Photographic Art Direction and Design	Miranda Harvey
Senior Art Editor	Susan Downing
Senior Editor	Dawn Henderson
Project Art Editor	Caroline de Souza
Designer	Elaine Hewson
Editorial Assistant	Ariane Durkin
DTP Designer	Traci Salter
Photographer	Jason Lowe
Food Stylist	Valerie Berry
Props Stylist	Wei Tang

First American Edition, 2007

Published in the United States by
DK Publishing
375 Hudson Street
New York, New York 10014

07 08 09 10 11   10 9 8 7 6 5 4 3 2 1

[PD180–August 2007]

Published in Great Britain by Dorling Kindersley Limited.

A catalog record for this book is available from
The Library of Congress.

ISBN 978-0-7566-2845-1

Color reproduction by MDP, UK
Printed and bound by Star Standard, Singapore

Discover more at
www.dk.com

contents

Introduction

Few can resist the magic of Provence—the Mediterranean sea shimmering in the distance between scented hills, the promise of a rosy dawn, and the peace of the landscape at night when even the cicadas become silent. If the appeal of the land needs no introduction, the riches of the food of the region are worth discovering, or rediscovering. Just as Provence tended to be the first southern port of call for visitors from northern Europe or from across the Atlantic, the cooking of Provence was the first Mediterranean cuisine to become fashionable. But trends move on swiftly and, in the last two or three decades, as other destinations and other cuisines came into the limelight, the dishes of the region became unfairly neglected.

I use the word "unfairly" advisedly. Provence food at its most authentic exemplifies the best of country cooking. It is simple, unpretentious, and sensible. It makes the best possible use of the ingredients of the land and of the sea. Where Provençal cuisine has been truly blessed is in the climate of the region and in its long Mediterranean coastline. Provence has always been a land of fragrant herbs, citrus and other fruit, sun-ripened vegetables, olives, pine nuts, and abundant fish and seafood. If anything, for our spoiled and demanding modern palates used to global culinary influences, the traditional Provençal cooking of old probably erred on the side of frugality. Waste was and still remains something any self-respecting Provençal cook intensely dislikes.

The success of a cookery school depends on a number of things, including a good location and enough creature comforts to satisfy the students, but the heart of the school, what makes it work, always is the chef—the teacher. When we started planning this book, our problem wasn't to find a place with *en suite* bathrooms and a state of the art kitchen, as it would have been for a real school. Everything instead hinged on finding the right chef. The person we were looking for had to be a genuine expert in traditional Provençal cooking, someone with a thorough knowledge of the recipes and the enthusiasm to make their background come alive. This person also had to have practical teaching experience and had to be able to understand the needs (and limitations) of home cooks in kitchens far away from Provence. Our ideal candidate also had to be able to explain unique local ingredients and inspire his audience about them, while at the same time keeping an open mind about suggesting the occasional substitute to encourage and enable people to cook *à la provençale* away from Provence.

Gui Gedda's name soon started coming up in many different places once I began my research. He was mentioned by several professional contacts and various friends. People described him as the guru of Provence food. I knew he had written books and I had heard of the detour-worthy authentic Provençal restaurant he ran for many years in Bormes-les-Mimosas above Le Lavandou (look up a map of the region and you'll find this between Saint Tropez and Toulon). He had also devised and taught cookery courses, and so met our criteria.

The concept of this book is simple. It introduces—or reintroduces—the food and cooking of Provence by telling the story of a week at a cookery school. Rather than traditional chapters, the contents, the "syllabus," are broken up into seven days. Each day deals with a

different aspect of Provençal food and cooking. The first day introduces the pantry ingredients, herbs, spices, and the *batterie de cuisine*—the cooking kit of the Provence home cook. Each day then focuses on a new subject: vegetables, sauces and eggs, meat and poultry, pasta and the pervasive Italian influence, fish and seafood, fruit, cheese and desserts. Gui introduces ingredients, explains techniques, and illustrates them with recipes. Recipes are very simple to start with and never difficult. They gradually get a little more complex as you, the student-reader, are encouraged to understand the favorite culinary techniques of Provence cooks, try different recipes, and build on your newly acquired skills.

In residential cookery courses not every hour is spent in the kitchen. There is plenty of time during the day to give students an opportunity to discover the markets, shops, and food producers of the region. This is reflected in this book by a number of "visits" to help you appreciate the exciting real produce and ingredients of Provence. You learn to shop the way the locals shop, at the same time as you learn to cook the way they cook. As well as getting a feel for good authentic produce and the best quality ingredients, you'll also discover that in the Provence kitchen a number of convenient shortcuts are acceptable—cold cuts of *charcuterie* for lunch, well-trimmed ready to cook meats, fresh bought bread, specialty cakes, and artisan preserves.

An old family friend of mine practically had tears in her eyes as she remembered Gui's stuffed sardines years after an early summer dinner at his restaurant. I practically have tears in my eyes when I remember my first meal with Gui. We had spent a long but enjoyable first working day together. We had had a frugal lunchtime snack of bread, fruit, and cheese, we had talked about the book and Provence cooking. We had discussed ingredients and dishes, as like-minded food lovers will do anywhere when they start talking about their favorite subject in earnest. The only time off he took, like a true Provençal, was for an early afternoon siesta, during which I slipped out to discover the pretty backstreets of Bormes and sip coffee on a terrace in the winter sunshine as I prepared my questions.

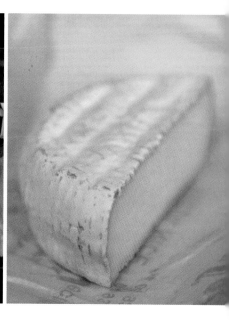

After we closed our files that evening I wanted to head back to the hotel for supper and leave him to a well-earned rest. *"Pas question,"* said Gui firmly. *"Tu dines ici"*—you are having dinner here. He gave me a glass of rosé and a warm slice of intensely flavored tomato tart (see recipe p288) as I watched him grill juicy chops of Sisteron lamb in the fireplace. He sprinkled them casually with a good pinch of coarse sea salt from a box he kept by the side of the fire. Hanging from the mantel over the hearth were strips of drying orange peel, ready to flavor Gui's daube, another of the many treats still to come during the days I spent working with him.

Gui's enthusiasm and knowledge were generous and contagious. He always made sure I understood fully what he had in mind. Thus we took a very early morning trip to the harbor fish market at Le Lavandou the day we discussed fish soup... It was January 3rd and still dark. Very few boats had been out, and the fishermen seemed to me to have that bleary hung over look you see everywhere for a day or two in wine-producing countries where they have just finished celebrating the new year. Gui was sprightlier than anyone and showed me every little fish there was to be seen before he taught me how to turn them into a succulent Soupe de Poissons. You'll find the recipe on page 268, and I hope you'll enjoy Gui's no-nonsense, sunny approach to food and cooking throughout the book.

Marie-Pierre Moine

monday

Welcome to the flavors of Provence. Meet your teacher, Gui Gedda. Discover the pantry ingredients and fresh aromatics Provençal cooks use to work their magic. Gui introduces his trusted *batterie de cuisine*—the basic kit you need to cook the recipes in this book. Apéritifs and a delicious dinner await at the end of the day.

Saveurs de Provence

It's tempting and all too easy to fill a Provençal pantry with good things in pretty jars and bottles, but these things are not just for decoration. Remember that every pot, can, or packet should work for its shelf space several times, and deliver its flavors before its expiration date arrives.

The best stocked and most useful pantries serve a dual purpose—basic ingredients, to enable the cook to concoct an emergency meal, and gourmet products to add a regional accent and flavor to everyday cooking.

The easiest way to make a dish conjure up the true taste of Provence is to cook it using the fat of the land—namely, olive oil. Stock two different oils—a basic olive oil for cooking and a more expensive extra virgin olive oil for last-minute drizzling. Keep extra virgin olive oil in a cool place, well away from direct sunlight. Resist the temptation to stock up—olive oil should be used within a year of being made, and within a few months of being purchased.

Give prominent shelf space to favorite local ingredients, such as anchovies, capers, coarse sea salt, olives, saffron, fruit preserves, canned tuna, sardines, and tomatoes. Spring cleaning a pantry twice a year is the best way to ensure you use every ingredient while it's in its prime—even flavored vinegars.

"Be ruthless. Taste and throw away anything that has become stale or simply no longer tastes how it's supposed to. If it doesn't taste right, it won't add anything to your cooking—it might even spoil a dish."

Dried goods

Dried beans, pasta, and rice are the core of the pantry and invaluable for cooking a hearty winter soup, substantial supper, or side dishes. Store dried goods in clear jars for easy identification. A "best used by" label on the lid is also helpful.

The long rice of Camargue is the only rice grown in France on a commercial scale. The grains are often red. Camargue rice is always of a very high quality, and in many cases organically grown.

Favorite lentils aren't grown in Provence—they are the small, green Puy lentils from the Auvergne. Less floury than most other lentils, they keep their nice firm texture during cooking.

Dried pasta is an essential standby. Provence cooks are fond of serving it as a side dish and use it at least as much as potatoes.

Pine nuts are the region's most popular nut. They have a lovely creamy taste, but since they are expensive they tend to be used sparingly.

Dried white and red beans are another useful staple. Perfect partners for other favorite Provence ingredients like garlic, herbs, and tomatoes, they often appear in stews, soups, and salads. Canned beans are also ubiquitous on cupboard shelves. A classic salad of the Nice region is made from canned tuna, drained and rinsed canned beans, and a good garlicky dressing with some chopped scallions.

Honey and preserves

If you traveled back in time 2,000 years to the land that is now Provence and found yourself in a room where food was stored, you would have found honey in an earthenware jar.

Honey has always been part of the culinary traditions of Provence and is a prized speciality of the region—there are now 500 registered beekeepers, of whom 350 make a living just from selling honey. For hundreds of years local beekeepers have been moving their hives to follow the seasons in their quest for nectar. Flavors vary from blends to single varieties, with lavender honey probably at the top of the list of favorite Provençal scented honeys. Lavender honey tends to be pale in color, aromatic, and supple—easy to spread and drizzle. It is perfect for breakfast and as an all-purpose scented sweetener. Other honey varieties for the pantry shelves are thyme, heather, rosemary, and *toutes fleurs* (mixed flowers).

Even if imports now make fresh fruit available throughout the year, preserving summer fruit for winter eating is a Provence tradition that refuses to disappear. Markets and specialist stores sell old-fashioned artisan jams, jellies, and bottled fruits that are guaranteed to look appealing on cupboard shelves—and to taste wonderfully fragrant and fruity alongside a piece of fresh bread for breakfast.

Flavorings and aromatics

The cooking of Provence is highly aromatic, with garlic playing an essential but surprisingly low-key role in most savory dishes—a leading player among a bouquet of fresh herbal flavors rather than the undisputed star of the show. Onions, occasionally with shallots, are often present in a supporting role.

Fresh flavors are at the heart of good Provençal food. Always use fresh garlic, onions, and shallots. Make the most of fresh herbs when they are available and use them liberally. The taste of fresh aromatic ingredients does not improve with age—it just loses its subtle and distinctive qualities, and becomes more assertive.

Come back from the market with as much garlic, shallots, onions, and fresh herbs as you'll need to prepare the next three or four meals, not what you are likely to require for the whole week. As well as tasting and smelling better, they'll be nicer to handle and work with—cooking with really fresh ingredients is always more satisfying than having to cut off dried-up or yellowing sections, or unwanted green shoots.

In season, treat yourself to a small fresh truffle, or even fresh truffle pieces—they may be very expensive, but they are without comparison. A good way to try a truffle is to store it with fresh eggs overnight. Use the eggs to make a moist, flat omelette. Just before slipping the omelette off the pan onto a plate, top with very thin truffle shavings.

"Just because we use garlic a lot does not mean that every dish is overwhelmed with a pungent garlicky taste. In good Provençal cooking, flavors can be intense but they are never overpowering."

Preparing garlic

Provence garlic comes in many shapes and sizes. Very fresh garlic resembles a large scallion (green onion) and has a mild flavor—good for slicing and grilling or roasting. Fresh garlic's purple-pink skin has the texture of slightly damp paper. Use the head whole and peel

Press The easiest way to separate a head of garlic into cloves is with your hands. For this to work the garlic has to be dry enough—if it's very young, the skin and flesh will be almost wet and sticky and you'll need a small, sharp knife.

after cooking and cooling, or peel and use individual cloves. Older garlic has drier papery skin and its cloves are good for crushing to a paste. Cloves sometimes have a green shoot in the center; remove this with the tip of a small knife before slicing, chopping, or crushing the garlic.

Twist Take hold of the head with both hands and turn in opposite directions while applying pressure with your fingers. Then all you have to do is to push the cloves with your thumbs to loosen and separate them.

Cut If your hands aren't strong enough to tear garlic, separate the cloves with the help of a small, sharp knife instead. Insert it in the ridge between two cloves and work it around gently until you have loosened off one clove. Don't prepare more garlic cloves than you need at one time—being attached to the head and protected by layers of papery skin keeps them fresh longer.

Making a bouquet garni

Making up the right bouquet garni for the dish you are preparing is a very important part of cooking *à la provençale*. Think of it as putting together a small corsage composed of the fragrant herbs most likely to enhance the flavor of the dish. A bouquet

Cut   Start with the core or base of the bouquet—an herb or vegetable strong enough to support the others. The best three are longish (1½–2½in /4–7cm) segments of celery or fennel, or a clean green leaf from a leek.

Pick   The classic herb combination is parsley and bay leaf or thyme. In Provence, a hint of anise flavor is added, usually with the help of fresh or dried fennel. For a rich meat dish, add celery and rosemary. For chicken or pork, replace the rosemary with tarragon or sage. For fish, try combining fennel, parsley, thyme, bay leaf, and dill.

garni should include a minimum of three herbs or aromatic vegetables, but use as many as you like. Add bouquets garnis to stews, roasts, and pot roasts at the end of the preparation stage, just before the cooking starts. Remove and discard the bouquet garni before serving.

Attach   Place your herbs on the vegetable base, then take a piece of kitchen string and tie it tightly around the bouquet. Celery and fresh fennel make perfect containers—you simply fill the hollow section with the herbs. If you are using a leek, lay the herbs halfway up the leaf and fold back the other half to enclose before tying.

Preparing anchovies

Small, silvery anchovies are enjoyed fresh during the summer months, but in Provençal cooking they are most often used cured. It is the curing, either in salt or in oil and salt, that gives them a special taste—salty, fishy, fermented—which adds a distinctive flavor

Lift out

Anchovies cured in salt are sold in glass jars or bottles. They tend to be larger in size and have a stronger flavor than anchovy fillets canned in oil. Use a clean fork to lift as many anchovies as you need from the jar.

to so many Mediterranean dishes. After opening a jar of anchovies, reseal it tightly and refrigerate; use the anchovies within 2 weeks. Leftover anchovies from a can should be transfered to a tightly covered jar or other container and kept in the refrigerator.

Rinse   When anchovies are packed in salt, much of the salt makes its way into their flesh. You need to get rid of all the visible salt to make the anchovies palatable. Rinse them in cold water, then drain well on a double layer of paper towels. There's no need to rinse anchovies canned in oil; simply pat dry with paper towels.

Mash   Curing softens anchovies, so they are easy to mash on a plate with the help of two forks. Mashing them means they will quickly melt into a dish, distributing their flavor evenly.

Pan bagna

Literally meaning "bathed bread," this is the original Provençal sandwich. It makes a perfect light dish or substantial snack. The secret is to use just-ripe tomatoes at room temperature so their juices will seep into the bread, and very fresh bread with a good crumb.

Serves 4

Preparation 10 minutes

6 medium vine-ripened tomatoes
white parts of 3 scallions
  (green onions)
4 medium eggs, hard-boiled
leaves from 1 small bunch of celery
½ small red bell pepper
about 16 small black olives
4 large, crusty white rolls

For the vinaigrette

6 anchovy fillets, packed in oil
  or salt
¾ cup olive oil
2½ tbsp red or white wine vinegar
fine sea salt and freshly ground
  black pepper to taste

Slice the tomatoes and the scallions. Peel the eggs, then slice crosswise. Coarsely chop the celery leaves. Core the red pepper and cut into thin strips. Pit the olives and leave whole or halve if you prefer.

To prepare the vinaigrette, drain or rinse the anchovy fillets and pat dry on paper towels. Chop or mash finely. Put them in a bowl or cup and add the olive oil and vinegar. Stir well and season with salt and pepper.

Slice the bread rolls horizontally in half and place the halves in front of you, cut sides up. Spread a generous spoonful of vinaigrette on the bottom half of each roll. Add the sliced tomatoes, red pepper strips, sliced scallions, egg, celery leaves, and black olives. Season lightly. Spoon the rest of the vinaigrette over the top.

Replace the top half of each roll. Working with one sandwich at a time, set a heavy plate on top and press down firmly but gently. Repeat with the remaining sandwiches. Let sit 5–10 minutes before cutting each sandwich in half to serve.

Give flavors time to develop, even if it's simple food like a sandwich. A lot of Provence dishes are best enjoyed at room temperature. Think of a terrace on a warm summer's evening…

Batterie de cuisine

The Provençal *batterie de cuisine*—the basic cooking equipment you need in the kitchen—is not very complicated. It reflects the traditional simplicity of the culinary tradition of this region of France.

In addition to a set of heavy-bottomed saucepans, you will need a solid, large, deep sauté pan with a lid, in enameled cast iron or copper. Frying pans should include one non-stick medium pan, preferably reserved for omelettes. A ridged grill pan is useful, especially when barbecuing or cooking in the hearth is not possible. If you have a barbecue or suitable hearth, you'll need a heavy wire cage-type grill for fish.

"The best equipment in the world cannot compete with a strong pair of hands and a little elbow grease."

In addition to colanders, sieves, and fine-meshed chinois, look for a round skimmer known as an *écumoire*. Use it for lifting ingredients out of cooking pots, and for removing surface sediment from cooking liquids.

You'll also need a set of good knives, a vegetable peeler, a chopping board, a grater, and a food mill (*mouli-légumes*).

The cookware specific to Provence are the *daubière*—the deep, glazed earthenware cooking pot in which daubes are traditionally cooked— and the gratin dishes also known as *tians*, which can be rectangular, oval, or round and should be as deep as possible.

A shallow olive wood bowl is ideal for serving salads. Provençal cooks traditionally prefer a mortar and pestle to a blender or food processor for pounding garlic and preparing thick sauces.

The pestle and mortar

No self-respecting Provençal cook's kitchen is complete without a well-worn pestle and mortar. The best mortars are made of marble or olive wood and they are much-loved pieces of equipment—often handed down from generation to generation. Gui Gedda's marble mortar was once used by his grandmother, although his olive wood pestle is relatively new.

A pestle and mortar is ideal for making garlicky sauces such as rouille (p118) and aïoli (p131). Once the garlic is crushed, other ingredients can be added and the pestle begins the job of pounding everything into a thick, sloppy mixture. The pounding gradually turns into beating, as the sauce becomes smoother, and you can start to move the pestle in circles as you would a whisk or wooden spoon.

"You might need to replace a pestle from time to time if you use it a lot, but a good mortar should last forever."

If you are investing in a pestle and mortar, be prepared to spend some money, and buy the largest available. The pestle and mortar is a very versatile tool. Its primary job is to crush garlic, often combined with salt, to a sticky coarse purée. It can also just as easily crush nuts, herbs, and spices. The mortar acts as a container and the pestle does the crushing and pounding.

dinner

Menu

apéritifs
roustides
d'anchois
-
omelette verte
-
brousse au miel
romarin

Apéritifs

L'apéritif is genuinely a happy hour in a day in Provence. It is the transition stage between the working hours and the evening, the moment when people relax with a drink and a nibble—*un amuse-bouche*—before dinner.

Made in Marseilles, and therefore authentically Provençal, Noilly Prat is a dry vermouth with a slightly salty, herbal tang. Served with plenty of ice, it's particularly good with green olives or green olive tapenade (p117).

No apéritif is complete without a savory bite to nibble on: radishes cut open and smeared with good butter, a dish of olives, or crisp toast spread with tapenade or anchovy paste (p116) are all popular.

Pastis is the supreme apéritif of Provence. It is made from anise and turns into a cloudy, opaque yellow when diluted with water and ice cubes. Some people think it tastes like toothpaste but its many fans believe it lifts the spirits and helps the digestion. The two best known brands are Ricard and Pernod and their respective fiercely loyal supporters always ask for "*un ricard*" or "*un pernod*" rather than *un pastis*. A dish of black olives makes a good nibble to serve with pastis.

Vin rosé

Whereas fruit and vegetables have always thrived in the Provence climate, in the past vines have tended not to fare so well under the strong sun, which can make grapes ripen too fast and thus produce excessively alcoholic wines. The science of winemaking has improved in the past 20 years and with it the quality of Provence wines. A growing number of small wineries are now producing well-made wines intended for drinking within two or three years rather than for aging.

The region of course produces fine red and white wines, but it is rosé that is the quintessential Provence wine. The wine of summer, the symbol of relaxed easy drinking, rosé is rapidly gaining popularity and cachet. As a wine, it is very versatile and a good multi-purpose choice. Rosé is equally at home as an apéritif as it is with a meal. It is meant to be drunk young and its fruity freshness makes it a good partner for vegetable, poultry, and white meat dishes. Dry rosé drinks well with fish and seafood, while slightly sweeter rosé can accompany cheese and fruit at the end of a meal.

Serve rosé lightly chilled rather than ice cold, to enjoy the bouquet and flavors.

Roustides d'anchois

Anchovy toasts well flavored with garlic, black pepper, and olive oil make a simply delicious appetizer and a perfect partner for a glass of chilled rosé wine. Anchovies have a strong salty taste and therefore should be used sparingly. They are also plentiful and inexpensive, which has made them a favorite staple ingredient and flavor-enhancer of thrifty Mediterranean cooks.

Serves 4

Preparation and cooking
  15 minutes
4 thick slices rustic bread
1 garlic clove, halved
4 anchovy fillets, packed in oil
  or salt
5 tbsp olive oil
½ tsp red or white wine vinegar
2 tsp finely chopped
  flat-leaf parsley
freshly ground black pepper
  to taste

Toast the bread until crisp and golden on both sides. Rub the toast on both sides with the cut sides of the garlic, spearing the garlic on a fork if you like. Set aside.

Drain or rinse the anchovy fillets and pat dry with paper towels. In a cup, mash the anchovy fillets, then add the olive oil and vinegar. Reserve 1 tsp parsley to finish, and add the rest to the cup. Stir to mix. Season with pepper.

Spread the anchovy mixture over one side of each toast. Let sit in a warm place such as the side of the hearth or a low oven for 2–3 minutes before sprinkling with the reserved chopped parsley. Serve at once.

Nothing beats an old-fashioned hearth for toasting bread, but you can of course use an oven, griddle, grill pan, or barbecue instead. Once toasted, rub well with garlic.

Omelette verte

Like other omelettes, a flat spinach omelette is not a difficult dish to prepare, but you need a dedicated omelette pan to cook it in, preferably non-stick and free of scratches. Cook the omelette until the egg is no longer runny: the spinach will help keep it moist. Serve with Tomates Provençale (p67).

Rinse the spinach without drying it; then put it in a non-stick sauté pan, sprinkle with a pinch of coarse salt, and stir over medium heat for 5 minutes until wilted. Turn the spinach into a colander. Let sit for 3–5 minutes until cool enough to handle, then press firmly with your hands to squeeze out moisture. Chop the spinach finely and reserve.

Finely chop the garlic with the parsley.

In a 9–10in (23–25cm) non-stick omelette pan, melt the butter over medium heat. Add the spinach and cook, stirring, until excess moisture has evaporated. Add the garlic and parsley, and cook for 1 minute. Remove from the heat.

Break the eggs into a bowl. Season with salt and pepper, then lightly whisk together to mix the eggs and yolks. Stir in the spinach mixture.

Wipe the pan clean with a paper towel. Return to medium–high heat and add half the oil. Lightly whisk the egg mixture, then pour half of it into the pan. Cook, shaking the pan back and forth over the heat and stirring to enable the egg mixture to spread out and set evenly.

Once the omelette is cooked, swirl a small piece of butter over it to make it shine. Slip into a heated dish, cover with a second dish, and keep warm while you cook the second omelette the same way. Cut the omelettes into wedges and serve as soon as possible. Makes 2 (9–10in) omelettes.

Serves 4

Preparation 10 minutes
Cooking 15 minutes
1¼lb (550g) baby spinach
coarse sea salt
1 large garlic clove, smashed
leaves from 3 sprigs of
 flat-leaf parsley
2½ tbsp unsalted butter, plus
 extra butter to finish
10 large eggs
fine sea salt and freshly ground
 black pepper to taste
2½ tbsp peanut oil

Rocking the sharp curved blade of a mezzaluna back and forth over the garlic and parsley makes quick work of chopping them.

Brousse au miel de romarin

Brousse is a fresh cheese made from whey, often bought as a large round weighing about 1lb (450g), enough for 4-6 people. It has a clean mild flavor and tastes less salty than most cheeses. Brousse may not be easy to find outside Provence, but very fresh ricotta makes a good alternative. Serve it simply—very fresh, with sweet grapes and rosemary-scented honey. Leftover Brousse can be added to pasta sauces or mixed with crème fraîche to serve with berries.

Remove the cheese from the refrigerator about 15 minutes before serving. Cut the cheese into wedges and put them on individual plates. (If you have any cheese left over, wrap in plastic wrap and refrigerate.)

Add a few grapes and a good drizzle of honey to each serving, then grind some black pepper over the top, if you like. Serve soon.

Variation

Rosemary honey is particularly good, but you might also want to try lavender or acacia honey.

Serves 4-6

Preparation 5 minutes
1lb (450g) fresh Brousse cheese
bunch of sweet grapes, rinsed
8–12 tbsp rosemary-scented
  clear honey
freshly ground black pepper
  to taste (optional)

Drizzle rosemary-scented honey
generously over the cheese, using
a honey dipper if you like.

tuesday

Today starts with a visit to a busy outdoor food market. In Provence as elsewhere there cannot be good cooking without top quality ingredients. Discover how to spot and pick the best locally grown vegetables. Learn the clever ways Provençal cooks have perfected to turn humble vegetables into simply exquisite dishes.

Au marché

Nowhere in France can beat the luxurious abundance of the market stalls of Provence. The region now shares its sun-ripened bounty with the rest of the country, but its produce is at its colorful best and freshest in local markets.

When you go to market, a good rule is to look out for vendors, both large and small, who make a point of prominently stressing the local origin of their produce. The short, mild winters and long, sunny summers of the Mediterranean climate have always provided the right conditions for growing vegetables and fruit. Local produce ripens early and well, and has a long and generous season. The beefsteak tomatoes grown in Provence are guaranteed to have plenty of flavor as well as the firm texture that makes them ideal for slicing.

If there's no mention of provenance, especially in winter or early in the spring, the produce may well be imported from Spain, Italy, or North Africa (and even from as far north as Holland, in the case of beefsteak tomatoes). If there a choice, it's always best to go for homegrown.

Get up early

Then you can enjoy a Provence market at its very best. Much of the top produce will be gone by 9:30 am. So set your alarm clock, draft a shopping list (be prepared to be flexible—the idea is to buy what's freshest and most appealing), and don't forget your shopping basket.

Walk through

Always spend a little time "casing the joint." Start with a quick walk through the market and let yourself be guided by your senses. It's always a good idea to compare the produce available at different stalls (or even in the same stall) before you buy.
▽

△
Touch

When you are buying salad greens, the varieties of leaves on display can be confusing. Handfuls of delicately different baby leaves and shoots are combined to make *mesclun*, the traditional mixed leaf salad of Provence. Mesclun varies from season to season and from stall to stall, each kind of salad leaf bringing its own taste and texture: peppery wild rocket (arugula), sweet chewy baby Oak Leaf, and bitter radicchio. Young leaves should feel light and fresh when you pick them up, not sticky or clumping together. If the vendor doesn't let you pick your own salad leaves, watch closely as he or she does this.

Look   Vivid orange, pale creamy green, sunny yellow, bright red, dark purple… sweet bell peppers add splashes of glorious color to Provence markets. Not surprisingly they are a favorite ingredient and local heroes of the region's cooking. Their flavor develops when they are charred or roasted, and being hollow yet sturdy makes them perfect for stuffing and baking.
▽

△
Smell   Remember the times you've been disappointed by perfect looking but totally bland supermarket produce. Bring vegetables and fruit near your nose, close your eyes, and concentrate on breathing in their aromas. Scallions should have a mild but unmistakable fresh oniony smell.

"Pick up what you're thinking of buying, feel its weight, and press gently to judge its texture. It doesn't matter if a vegetable or fruit looks a little less than perfectly shaped, as long as it feels just ripe."

Don't be shy Do you want to know where the tomatoes on display come from? Or how long to cook the green asparagus? The only way to find out is to ask. Even if you are hesitant about speaking French, you can point and inquire, and you'll always find someone to volunteer to be your interpreter.

Seek advice Unlike supermarket clerks, the people behind the counters are experts. More often than not, on smaller stalls they are also the producers, proud of what they are bringing to market and more than happy to talk about it and give cooking tips to customers.
▽

Cépes Secs
300€ kilo   Massif central
30€
les 100gr

△
Learn Of the many kinds of dried mushrooms available in Provence market stalls, dried porcini (cépes) are probably the most expensive, but their strong unique flavor makes them a reliable favorite. Choose thickly sliced, clean-looking, plump mushrooms; avoid overdried shriveled, small pieces. Before using them, soak in water for at least 20 minutes, and pick out any bits of straw or dirt.

Pick your own   Many market sellers are happy to let their customers help themselves. Take your time choosing. This will give you a chance to handle and smell the produce, to feel its weight and texture, and to check that its aroma is fresh and clean.

▽

△
Select with care
Even the most modest heap of vegetables is displayed with simple but mouthwatering flair. What you see is what you get: green asparagus is neatly stacked, making it easy for you to pick spears of identical size, which will take the same time to cook—very convenient once you are back in the kitchen.

"One of the secrets of good cooking is to shop little, but often. This way even simple dishes will taste fresh and at their best. And the more frequently you visit a market, the better the sellers will look after you!"

Preparing eggplant

Eggplants are magnificent, versatile vegetables. A natural partner for garlic and herbs, they are equally good baked, fried, grilled, and stewed, and you can serve them sliced, halved, puréed, or chopped. Their satisfying texture makes them ideal for meat-free

Pick   When you handle an eggplant, it should feel heavy in your hand. It should look unblemished, firm, and shiny. Check that the peduncle—at the stalk end—is green and spiky. If you are going to stuff eggplant halves, it helps if they are all the same size.

Trim   Cut off both ends, then slice the eggplant in half lengthwise. At this stage, if you like, you can sprinkle the cut sides lightly with coarse sea salt, place upside down on a clean tea towel, put a weight on top, and leave to drain for 30 minutes. This will help get rid of moisture and make the eggplants less oil-absorbent. Rinse and press gently to dry before using.

occasions. Their only downside is a tendency to absorb oil. Salting with coarse sea salt and then draining them—a technique known as *dégorger*—is a way of making them less oil-greedy and of avoiding any possible residual bitterness. It also improves their texture.

Score   Before grilling or roasting eggplants, score the flesh with the point of a sharp knife in a crisscross pattern. Take care not to pierce the skin. Drizzle the flesh with a little olive oil and season lightly with salt and pepper.

Drain   After frying eggplants, put them in a colander and press down firmly with an *écumoire* (a large, round, perforated skimmer or spatula) to get rid of excess fat and moisture. This makes the eggplant less heavy and finer tasting.

Fondue d'aubergine

Charring the skin of the eggplant gives this smooth dip a tantalizing smoky flavor. It makes a great appetizer served with crisp breadsticks, baked croûtons, or crudités. Also try it with slices of salami and olives as an informal little starter—on its own, or tapas-style. It will keep for 2-3 days when covered tightly with plastic wrap in the refrigerator.

Serves 4

Preparation 10 minutes
Cooking 40 minutes
1 large eggplant
fine sea salt and freshly ground
   black pepper to taste
juice of ½ lemon
1 garlic clove, crushed
½ tsp ground cumin (optional)
1 roasted tomato (see Tomates
   Provençale, p67)
2 tbsp extra virgin olive oil

Preheat the oven to 375°F/190°C.

Spear the eggplant on a long-handled fork or barbecue skewer. Carefully char over a gas burner for a couple of minutes, turning the eggplant to lightly brown the skin a little all over. If you do not have a gas cooktop, char the eggplant in a grill pan or broiler, turning it carefully with tongs.

Line a baking sheet with parchment paper. Put the charred eggplant on the baking sheet and pierce a few times with a fork. Bake for about 30 minutes, turning it over after 15 minutes. Check the eggplant for tenderness by piercing it with a fork.

Set aside the eggplant until cool enough to handle, then slice it in half lengthwise. Scoop out the flesh with a tablespoon and put the flesh in a sieve. Sprinkle lightly with salt and press down firmly to remove excess moisture.

Put the eggplant in a food processor and add the lemon juice, garlic, cumin, and tomato. Pulse quickly to mix together until just smooth. Do not overblend. Taste the purée and season lightly with salt and pepper.

Transfer the eggplant to a serving bowl. Swirl the olive oil over the top just before serving at room temperature.

"If you haven't got a spare roast tomato, you can replace it with a couple of small cherry tomatoes."

Papeton d'aubergine

Eggplant mousse has a milder flavor and creamier texture than its country cousin, the eggplant dip on the opposite page. You can prepare the mousse ahead and chill it, to serve as a chic dinner party starter. If you make the mousse in advance, be sure to give it time to return to room temperature before serving—if it's too cold the flavors will be hidden.

Preheat the oven to 375°F/190°C. Line a baking sheet with parchment paper. Cut the eggplants in half lengthwise and score the flesh with a crisscross pattern (see p61). Place cut sides up on the prepared sheet. Brush with a little oil. Bake for about 20 minutes or until tender.

Meanwhile, char and peel the red pepper (see p65); remove the seeds and finely chop the flesh. Heat 1 tbsp of the oil in a sauté pan over a low heat, add the onion and garlic, and cook, stirring, until the onion is just tender and translucent but not browned. Set aside.

Remove the eggplants from the baking sheet and let sit until cool enough to handle. Scoop out the flesh with a tablespoon and chop finely. Add the eggplant and red pepper to the onion mixture, season to taste, and stir in the crème fraîche. Cook over medium heat for 5 minutes, stirring occasionally. Let cool to room temperature before serving.

Mix the remaining 4 tbsp olive oil with the vinegar to make a dressing. Season lightly with salt and pepper.

Spoon a little mound of eggplant mousse in the center of each of 4 plates. Arrange the salad leaves around the mousse and drizzle with the dressing. Garnish with the basil and serve at once.

Serves 4-6

Preparation 20 minutes
Cooking 30 minutes
2 eggplants
5 tbsp olive oil, plus extra
   for brushing
½ red bell pepper
½ red onion, finely chopped
1 garlic clove, crushed
fine sea salt and freshly ground
   black pepper to taste
1 heaping tbsp crème fraîche
1 tbsp red or white wine vinegar
3 cups baby salad leaves
a few fresh basil leaves to garnish

Ratatouille

This is slow cooking Provence-style—a perfect dish to cook quietly in the afternoon, when it's too hot to go out. Ratatouille comes from the words *rata*, which means grub, and *touiller*, to stir. Its name may be humble but a proper ratatouille is a glorious medley of tender vegetables. You can't prepare it in a hurry, so make plenty and enjoy the leftovers. Turn the page for inspiration.

Heat a large frying pan, add 3 tbsp oil, and cook the onions over a medium–low heat, stirring frequently, for 12–15 minutes or until soft and golden. Season with salt and pepper. Drain well in a colander. Wipe out the large frying pan and set aside.

Char and peel the peppers, remove the seeds, and cut the flesh into 1½in (4cm) squares. Heat another frying pan, add 2 tbsp oil, and cook the peppers over medium heat for 3–4 minutes or until softened. Drain well in a colander. Wipe out this second frying pan and set aside.

Blanch and skin the tomatoes (see p90), and cut into quarters. Put them in a large sauté pan, drizzle with 3 tbsp oil, and add the bouquet garni and garlic. Season with salt and pepper and stir in the sugar. Cook over a medium heat for 20 minutes.

Meanwhile, cut the zucchini and eggplants into cubes. Add 3 tbsp oil to the large frying pan and cook the zucchini over a medium heat for 6–8 minutes or until soft. Lift out with a slotted spoon and drain on paper towels.

Heat the second frying pan. Add 3 tbsp oil and cook the eggplants over medium heat for 6–8 minutes or until softened. Drain in a colander, pressing out excess oil.

Add all the drained vegetables to the tomatoes. Stir in ⅔ cup water and season with salt and pepper. Cover and cook over low heat for 20 minutes, stirring occasionally. Remove the bouquet garni, adjust the seasonings, and stir in the basil.

Serves 8

Preparation and cooking
  3 hours
14 tbsp olive oil
2lb (900g) large onions, sliced
fine sea salt and freshly ground
  black pepper to taste
3 red bell peppers
2lb (900g) ripe tomatoes or
  drained canned tomatoes
1 bouquet garni, made with a
  celery stick and 2 bay leaves
  (pp28–29)
9 garlic cloves, crushed
pinch of sugar
3lb (1.3kg) zucchini
1lb (450g) eggplant
6 fresh basil leaves, chopped

Firmly spear each pepper on a fork and turn it over a gas flame until dark and blistered all over. Cool for a couple of minutes, then rinse and rub off the charred skin.

Suggestions pour ratatouille

Ratatouille au bœuf

Chop about ¼lb (115g) leftover beef from a daube (see p192) and stir into 1¼ cups ratatouille. Add ½ tsp fresh thyme leaves. Reheat gently. Serves 2 as a light supper.

Ratatouille piquante

Stir 4 chopped fresh mint leaves and 1 tbsp red or white wine vinegar into 1½ cups cold ratatouille. Adjust the seasonings. Scatter 12 small black olives over the top. Serve as an appetizer with toasted baguette, or with cold chicken, veal, or ham. Serves 4–6.

Ratatouille et pommes de terre

Peel and quarter a large, waxy potato. Cook in salted boiling water until just tender. Drain and refresh under cold running water. Stir into 1½ cups ratatouille. Add 3 tbsp water and reheat gently. Stir in a finely chopped scallion and 1 tbsp chopped fresh flat-leaf parsley. Serves 2 as a side dish.

Œufs à la ratatouille

Hard-boil 6 large eggs. Peel and cut in half lengthwise. Scoop out the yolks and mash coarsely with a fork. Reserve 1 tbsp; gently stir the rest into ½ cup cold ratatouille with 2 tsp chopped capers and 1 tsp finely grated lemon zest. Fill the egg white halves with the mixture and top each with a little of the reserved yolk. Serves 6–8 as part of an assortment of cold appetizers.

Riz à la ratatouille

Make Riz Pilaf (p292), but don't stir in the extra butter. Spread the rice in a gratin dish. Spoon 1 cup ratatouille over the rice, spreading it evenly. Sprinkle with 6 tbsp shredded Gruyère cheese. Bake in a preheated 400°F/200°C oven for 8–12 minutes until bubbling-hot. Serves 6 as a main dish.

Baguette brouillade à la ratatouille

Cut a baguette crosswise into 4 equal pieces. Split open each piece, and lightly toast the cut sides under a broiler. In a large sauté pan, melt 3 tbsp unsalted butter. Break 6 eggs into a bowl, season lightly, and stir to break the yolks. Add the eggs to the pan and stir over medium heat until scrambled and just set. Stir in ¼ cup ratatouille and spoon the mixture over the cut sides of the baguette. Loosely roll up 2–3 slices of cured ham and cut into small ribbons. Distribute over the egg topping and broil until piping hot. Serves 4 as a brunch or supper.

Tomates provençale

Slow roasting brings out the natural sweetness of tomatoes. Since they make a great side dish, it's a good idea to roast more tomatoes than you need for a recipe—double the quantity and use what's left to make a sauce or to serve with roast chicken, grilled fish, or lamb cutlets another day.

Preheat the oven to 375°F/190°C.

Halve the tomatoes. Scoop out the seeds, then put the tomato halves in a colander cut side down, pressing down gently with the palm of your hand. Let drain in the sink or over a plate for 5 minutes, or longer if convenient.

Lightly oil a gratin dish just large enough to hold the halved tomatoes in a single layer. Put the tomatoes in the dish, cut sides facing up. Sprinkle with the olive oil. Season lightly with salt, pepper, marjoram, and sugar—using the same quantity of sugar as salt.

Bake for about 1 hour. Let cool for a few minutes before serving. The tomatoes can be refrigerated for 2 or 3 days, or frozen for up to 1 month.

Serves 4

Preparation 15 minutes
Cooking 1 hour

8 ripe but firm, medium to large
    vine-ripened tomatoes
1 tbsp olive oil, plus extra
    for greasing
fine sea salt and freshly ground
    black pepper to taste
sugar
2 tsp dried marjoram or oregano
    leaves

"Serve the roasted tomatoes warm or at room temperature rather than piping hot, so you can really appreciate their sweet flavor."

Beignets de courgettes

With their crisp batter, zucchini fritters make a good side dish for fish and white meat entrées. Once fried, the fritters can be kept hot for 20 minutes in the oven, uncovered, on a clean towel or a double layer of paper towels.

Serves 4-6

Preparation and cooking about 40 minutes, plus resting and draining 2 hours

2lb (900g) zucchini

¾ cup peanut oil

For the batter

1¼ cups plain flour

1 tbsp olive oil

fine sea salt and freshly ground black pepper to taste

2 large eggs

⅔ cup milk

To prepare the batter, sift the flour into a bowl, add the olive oil, and season with a generous pinch of salt and a good grinding of pepper. Separate the eggs, reserving the whites in a separate mixing bowl. Add the yolks and the milk to the flour and stir well to mix. Cover and let rest for 2 hours.

While the batter is resting, cut the zucchini into small dice. Heat ¼ cup of the peanut oil in a large sauté pan. Add the zucchini, stir, and cover the pan. Cook over low heat for 10 minutes until soft, stirring from time to time. Turn the zucchini into a colander and let drain for 1 hour to remove the excess oil.

Whisk the egg whites until small peaks form. Gently fold them into the batter; then carefully stir in the drained zucchini and season with pepper.

Wipe the sauté pan clean with paper towels. Add the remaining ½ cup peanut oil and heat until very hot. Line a platter with a double layer of paper towels. Working in batches, add one-quarter of the zucchini batter in small spoonfuls to the hot oil. Cook over a fairly high heat for 2–3 minutes until golden all over, turning halfway through cooking. Lift out with a slotted spoon and drain on the paper towels.

Repeat with the remaining batter in 3 more batches, lowering the heat a bit if the oil gets too hot and starts smoking. Drain as before. Serve the fritters hot.

Carefully mix the zucchini into the batter, then drop spoonfuls into the hot oil to fry, turning once, until they are crisp and golden.

Pistou

Orange-colored Mimolette cheese gives this sauce an unusual color and a mildly nutty sweet flavor that balances the peppery basil. Instead of Mimolette you could use mature Edam, Gruyère, or Cheddar cheese. The sauce is essential in Soupe au Pistou (p73). Also use it to dress pasta, stir it into plain boiled rice, or serve it as a dip for crudités or a topping for baked croûtons.

Makes about 1¼ cups

Preparation 20 minutes

6 garlic cloves
coarse sea salt to taste
leaves from 2 large handfuls
   of fresh basil
3 medium, vine-ripened tomatoes
freshly ground black pepper
   to taste
2oz (55g) Mimolette cheese
⅓ cup olive oil

Smash and peel the garlic, then put it in a mortar. Season with a little coarse sea salt. Pound the garlic with the pestle until coarsely crushed.

Tear up the basil leaves and add half to the mortar with a little more salt. Stir in and pound until well mixed. Add the rest of the basil and continue pounding until you have a *pommade* (a thick purée).

Blanch and skin the tomatoes (see p90); remove the seeds and chop the flesh. Gradually work the tomatoes into the *pommade*, pounding, until it loosens and you have a thick sauce. Season with pepper.

Grate the cheese and mix into the sauce. Add the oil, mixing well. Adjust the seasoning. The sauce will keep for up to 3 days, refrigerated in a bowl covered tightly with plastic wrap.

"Making pistou is very satisfying! First pound down to crush the mixture, then stir, always going in the same direction. You'll know the sauce is ready when it makes a nice sloshy sound in the mortar. Once you've stirred in the cheese, the texture will be like mayonnaise."

Soupe au pistou

This rustic soup owes its body and substance to beans. If at all possible use fresh beans in the shell—they are well worth buying when they appear in markets in the early summer. Fresh beans cook more quickly than dried, and are lighter and easier to digest. To make the most of their short season, freeze them after boiling for 20 minutes, draining, rinsing, and cooling.

Put 7 cups cold water in a large soup pot. Add the ham hock. Bring to a simmer, then partially cover and let bubble gently for 30 minutes while you prepare the vegetables. Skim occasionally to remove any foam that rises to the top.

Shell the white and red beans. Put them in a saucepan, cover with plenty of cold water, and bring to a boil. Simmer for 10 minutes, then drain and refresh under cold running water. While the beans are simmering, trim the green beans, then cut crosswise into bite-size pieces. Peel and dice the potatoes. Blanch and skin the tomatoes (see p90); remove the seeds and chop the flesh. Chop the zucchini.

Add all the vegetables to the soup pot. Season lightly. Return to a simmer, then cook, partially covered, for 1 hour, skimming occasionally.

Test that the ham hock and beans are tender when pierced with a fork. Remove the ham hock, take the meat from the bone, shred, and reserve. Lift half of the ingredients out of the pan with a small sieve or large slotted spoon and put on a plate. Mash gently with a fork, then return to the soup along with the shredded ham.

Add the macaroni. Increase the heat and cook until the pasta is just tender to the bite. Adjust the seasoning. Remove from the heat, stir in the pistou, and serve.

Variation
Instead of fresh haricot beans, you can use two 15oz (450g) cans cannellini beans, drained and rinsed. Increase the cooking time for the ham hock to 50 minutes, then add the beans with all the vegetables and cook for 30 minutes.

Serves 6-8

Preparation 30 minutes
Cooking 1½ hours
1 ham hock, or a thick piece
   of smoked bacon, about
   6oz (175g)
½lb (225g) fresh white beans, such
   as cannellini or flageolet
¼lb (115g) fresh red beans, such
   as borlotti
½lb (225g) Italian flat green beans
2 medium russet potatoes
3 tomatoes
4 medium zucchini
fine sea salt and freshly ground
   black pepper to taste
¼lb (115g) small macaroni or
   other pasta
⅔ cup Pistou (p70)

Fresh beans do not need to be soaked, nor do they need long cooking to make them perfectly tender. After draining them in a colander, run cold water over them to rinse and refresh.

Haricots verts à la provençale

Tiny french green beans are one of the many treats of the Provence summer. They are fine and extremely tender, and need only a little olive oil, butter, parsley, and garlic to turn them into a veritable feast. This is a versatile side dish, also worth featuring on its own as an appetizer.

Serves 4

Preparation 10 minutes
Cooking 5-7 minutes
1lb (450g) tender, young
   green beans (haricots verts)
1 tbsp olive oil
1 garlic clove, crushed
leaves from 6 sprigs of flat-leaf
   parsley, finely chopped
2 tbsp unsalted butter, cut into bits
fine sea salt and freshly ground
   black pepper to taste

Bring a large saucepan of water to a boil. Season generously with salt. Trim the beans, then add to the boiling water and cook 1–5 minutes, depending on their size. They should be tender but not soft. Turn the beans into a colander, refresh with very cold water, and drain well.

Return the pan to low heat, add the olive oil and garlic, and cook, stirring, for about 1 minute to soften. Add the drained beans, turn up the heat, and add the parsley. Cook, stirring, for 1 minute or until heated through.

Turn into a warm serving dish. Stir in the butter, adjust the seasonings, and serve.

Salade de haricots verts

Stop cooking the beans a minute or two earlier, when they are no longer crunchy but still firm. Drain and refresh under cold running water. In a small frying pan, cook the garlic in 2 tbsp olive oil over low heat until soft, then add to the beans with the parsley. Let sit until cool, then stir in a little more olive oil and 1–2 tsp lemon juice or red or white wine vinegar.

Fenouil aux olives

Fennel parcels with olives make a good accompaniment for baked or barbecued fish, or they can be served on their own as an appetizer. The dish is cooked in two stages—first steaming to make the fennel and vegetables tender, then baking in foil with parsley and orange zest to develop the flavors. Black olives and extra virgin olive oil add a Mediterranean flourish.

Trim the fennel bulbs, then quarter each one lengthwise. Bring water to a boil in the bottom of a steamer. Put the fennel, onion, garlic, and shallot in the top of the steamer. Cover and cook for 10 minutes or until crisp-tender.

Preheat the oven to 400°F/200°C. Cut 4 pieces of foil, each large enough to hold one-quarter of the mixture in the steamer.

Divide the fennel mixture among the pieces of foil. Add the parsley and orange zest, and season with salt and pepper. Drizzle 1 tbsp oil over each portion of vegetables and wrap to make parcels, making sure the edges are sealed tightly. Put the parcels on a baking sheet, sealed edges facing up, and bake for 20 minutes.

While the parcels are in the oven, pit and chop the olives. Put them in a cup, season with a little pepper, and stir in the remaining 1 tbsp olive oil.

Slit open the parcels without unwrapping completely, add a bit of the olive mixture to each, and serve.

Serves 4

Preparation 15 minutes
Cooking 30 minutes
3 large fennel bulbs
1 onion, thinly sliced
3 garlic cloves, sliced
1 shallot, thinly sliced
2 tbsp finely chopped
   flat-leaf parsley
1 tbsp finely grated orange zest
fine sea salt and freshly ground
   black pepper to taste
5 tbsp extra virgin olive oil
8 black kalamata or other
   flavorful olives

"Go easy on the salt—remember that olives are salty."

Carottes à la crème d'olives vertes

Slow cooking brings out the sweet tenderness of carrots. Keep the heat moderate and don't be tempted to rush the cooking, or you will end up with tough, burnt carrots. The slightly bitter taste of green olives adds a good finishing touch.

Serves 6

Preparation 15 minutes
Cooking 50 minutes
2lb (900g) carrots
½ cup peanut oil
⅓ cup green olives
2 garlic cloves, smashed
leaves from 4 sprigs of
  flat-leaf parsley
1 tbsp soft unsalted butter
fine sea salt and freshly ground
  black pepper to taste
½ cup light cream or half-and-half

Peel the carrots and cut into matchstick-size pieces.

Place a large non-stick frying pan over medium–low heat. Once the pan is hot, add the oil. Cook the carrots very gently and slowly, turning and stirring frequently—allow 35 minutes for the carrots to be cooked through and tender.

Meanwhile, put the olives in a saucepan, cover with boiling water, and cook for 2 minutes. Drain in a colander. Discard the pits and chop the olive flesh with the garlic and parsley.

Turn the cooked carrots into a colander and let drain for 30 minutes, stirring them a few times.

Melt the butter in a sauté pan over medium heat. Add the olive mixture and stir for a minute. Add the carrots and stir well for 2–3 minutes. Season, then add the light cream and cook for 5 minutes, stirring a few times.

Stir in ⅔ cup water. Reduce the heat to low and cook for 10 minutes, stirring several times. Serve piping hot in a warmed shallow bowl.

Aspergeade

White, green, or purple—and wild—asparagus thrives in Provence during the spring. Green asparagus, with its distinctive flavor, is best used to prepare this appetizer. It will look good on a buffet, but you can also divide the asparagus and the creamy dipping sauce among individual plates.

Bring a wide sauté pan of lightly salted water to a boil. Meanwhile, carefully peel the stalks of the asparagus and rinse. Cut off the woody ends and drop them into the simmering water. Return the water to a boil, then lower the heat a little and simmer for 5 minutes.

Add the asparagus spears and simmer for 5–8 minutes until just tender when pierced with a fork. The timing will depend on the thickness of the asparagus spears—check after 5 minutes.

Drain, reserving a few tablespoons of cooking liquid. Refresh under cold water and drain again. Set the asparagus spears aside on a clean cloth or double layer of paper towels. Reserve the woody ends.

In a blender or food processor, mix together the lemon zest and juice, mustard, egg yolk, and cooked asparagus ends with a little salt and pepper to season. With the motor running, slowly trickle in the peanut oil, and then the olive oil. Taste and adjust the seasoning. The sauce should be thick but not solid. If necessary, beat in 1 tbsp of the asparagus cooking liquid to loosen it a little. When making ahead, cover and chill until ready to serve.

Put the sauce in the center of a shallow serving bowl and arrange the asparagus spears around it, tips facing in. Snip the chives and parsley, sprinkle over the top, and serve soon.

Serves 4

Preparation 15 minutes
Cooking 15 minutes
12 thick green asparagus spears
finely grated zest and juice
   of ½ juicy lemon
½ tsp Dijon mustard
1 medium egg yolk
fine sea salt and freshly ground
   black pepper to taste
¼ cup peanut or sunflower oil
¼ cup olive oil
6 fresh chives
leaves from 2 sprigs of fresh
   flat-leaf parsley

"The sauce might thicken if you put it in the refrigerator, so save a little of the cooking liquid to dilute it after chilling. There's no need to chill the asparagus if you prepare the dish a few hours ahead. Just cover and keep in a cool place."

Les tomates

Cooks in Provence are so fond of tomatoes that they affectionately call them *pommes d'amour*, the apples of love. A relative newcomer to the region, tomatoes have thrived in the warm sun and become so well entrenched and ubiquitous that they are now a cornerstone of traditional Provençal cuisine.

The Provence climate suits tomatoes perfectly, and locally grown tomatoes are unlikely to taste blandly disappointing. For eating raw, look out for newly ripe tomatoes. They'll have a little crunch to their texture, no real acidity, and a faint, fresh grassy-green aroma, particularly if they are still on the vine or have just been picked.

For cooking and sauces, choose firm, bright red tomatoes at their peak of ripeness. It doesn't matter if they are a little misshapen. For stuffing, choose tomatoes with a slightly thicker skin—the elongated varieties are excellent for halving and filling. If you are going to scoop out the flesh and leave the casing whole, select tomatoes that can stand upright.

Beware of overripe soft tomatoes—they will have a squishy, watery texture, too much acidity, and little or no flavor.

"Even beefsteak tomatoes, not normally praised for their flavor will taste luscious and full of sun when they have ripened in Provence."

Tomates farcies

Stuffing vegetables with leftover meat or rice and plenty of aromatic flavorings is a favorite cooking method of thrift-conscious Provençal cooks. Stuffed tomatoes are probably the most popular of all the *farcis*. You need to use firm rather than ripe tomatoes to make sure they don't collapse during cooking. Serve as an appetizer, or with Riz Pilaf (p292) or pasta as a main course.

Serves 6

Preparation 30 minutes
Cooking 1½ hours

12 fairly large, firm tomatoes
fine sea salt and freshly ground
   black pepper to taste
3 tbsp olive oil, plus extra for
   greasing
1 large mild onion, finely chopped
2 garlic cloves, crushed
leaves from 5 sprigs of flat-leaf
   parsley, finely chopped
8 fresh basil leaves, finely chopped
2 bay leaves
6oz (175g) ham or leftover cooked
   meat, finely chopped
2 medium eggs

Cut a lid from the stalk end of each tomato and reserve. If necessary, trim the base to enable the tomato to stand upright. Using a teaspoon, cut out the flesh and pulp without breaking the skin. Reserve the flesh; discard the seeds and white parts. Season the insides of the tomatoes with a little salt, then turn them upside down in a large colander to drain while you prepare the stuffing.

Preheat the oven to 400°F/200°C. Lightly oil one or two gratin dishes large enough to hold the tomatoes side by side.

Place a large frying pan over medium heat. Once the pan is hot, add the oil, then add the onion and cook for 7–10 minutes, stirring occasionally, until softened but not browned. Stir in the garlic, parsley, and basil, then add the reserved tomato flesh and the bay leaves. Cook for 5 minutes, stirring occasionally. Add the ham and cook for 2 minutes longer. Remove from the heat.

Discard the bay leaves. Whisk the egg lightly just to mix the yolks and whites. Add to the stuffing mixture. Season with salt and pepper. Using a teaspoon, stuff the tomatoes, leaving a little room at the top. Arrange them in the gratin dishes and top with the reserved tomato lids. Loosely cover with foil and bake for 1 hour. Let cool for a few minutes before eating.

Variations

Use the same method and filling for stuffed red peppers (*poivrons farcis*). The filling can also be used for other vegetables, but before you stuff them, you will need to parboil onions and potatoes, and bake zucchini—the round ones are ideal—and eggplants.

Salt the hollowed-out tomatoes, then set aside to drain out the excess juices that could make the baked tomatoes soggy.

Tian aux courgettes

Zucchini gratin makes a simple yet satisfying main course. Serve it with a side salad, and some cured ham or salami for diehard carnivores. You can follow exactly the same recipe to prepare an eggplant gratin.

Serves 6

Preparation 20 minutes,
 plus draining
Cooking 1¼ hours
4½lb (2kg) zucchini
¼ cup olive oil
4oz (115g) Gruyère cheese,
 shredded (about 1 cup)
½ cup light cream or half-and-half
½ tsp grated fresh nutmeg
1 tsp dried sage leaves
fine sea salt and freshly ground
 black pepper to taste

Dice the zucchini, then put them in a soup pot or very large saucepan with the oil. Cover and cook over medium heat for 15–20 minutes or until tender, stirring occasionally. Turn the zucchini into a colander and let sit for 30 minutes to drain off the excess moisture.

Preheat the oven to 400°F/200°C.

Gently press down the drained zucchini with the flat side of a wide slotted spoon to be sure they are well drained, then transfer to a *tian* or gratin dish. Add half the grated cheese, the cream, nutmeg, and sage, and stir to mix. Season with salt and pepper. Spread out and smooth the surface with the back of a fork. Sprinkle with the remaining cheese. Bake for 15–20 minutes until golden. Serve hot.

Trim the stalk end from the zucchini, then cut them into small, neat pieces about the same size to ensure they will cook evenly.

Tian de pommes de terre

Well flavored with garlic and enriched with cream, this potato gratin is a modern version of a frugal dish of old Provence called *lou tian de poumo*—potatoes cooked in the hearth in a garlic-rubbed pan.

Serves 6

Preparation 30 minutes
Cooking 50 minutes
3lb (1.35kg) large waxy potatoes
6 garlic cloves, smashed
leaves from 6 sprigs of flat-leaf
    parsley, plus extra chopped
    parsley to garnish
2 tbsp unsalted butter
1 tsp fresh thyme leaves, chopped
½ cup milk
½ cup light cream or half-and-half
⅔ cup Gruyère cheese, shredded
½ tsp grated fresh nutmeg
fine sea salt and freshly ground
    black pepper to taste

Preheat the oven to 400°F/200°C. Lightly grease a *tian* or gratin dish.

Bring plenty of lightly salted water to a boil in a large saucepan. Peel the potatoes and cut into ½in (1cm) slices. Add them to the pan, return to a boil, and continue boiling gently for 15 minutes, stirring from time to time. The potatoes should be almost cooked but still a little firm. Drain in a colander.

While the potatoes are cooking, finely chop together the garlic and parsley. Melt the butter in a medium saucepan, add the garlic and parsley and the thyme, and stir over medium heat for 2 minutes. Stir in the milk and cream. Bring to a boil, then immediately remove from the heat. Stir in half the cheese and the nutmeg. Season with a little salt and plenty of pepper.

Spread the potato slices in the gratin dish and spoon the cream and cheese sauce over the top. Top with the remaining cheese. Bake for 30 minutes or until golden brown on top. Serve hot, sprinkled with parsley.

Tian de pommes de terre et aux champignons

For a deeper flavored gratin, soak ¾oz (20g) dried mushrooms in very hot water for 15 minutes to plump them up, then drain and chop. Add to the potatoes together with a drained, chopped anchovy fillet before baking.

Cardons aux anchois

Cardoons are a winter vegetable related to artichokes, but with edible ribs that look a little like celery stalks. They need to be carefully cleaned and cooked. Their lovely delicate flavor goes well with anchovy sauce.

Bring a large saucepan of salted water to a boil. Meanwhile, prepare the cardoons. Put half of the lemon juice in a bowl of cold water. Remove the prickly leaves and roots from the cardoons. Cut the cardoon stalks into 2in (5cm) pieces, removing any stringy filaments, and add to the bowl of lemon water as you cut them, to prevent them from discoloring.

Add the rest of the lemon juice and the bouquet garni to the pan of boiling water. Drain the cardoons and add to the pan. Return to a gentle rolling boil and cook for 25 minutes or until tender. Drain the cardoons and set aside. Reserve the cooking liquid, discarding the bouquet garni.

To make the sauce, put half the olive oil in a saucepan, add the flour, and stir over medium heat for 2 minutes until just golden. Add the anchovies and garlic and cook, stirring, for 1 minute. Gradually stir in about 1 cup of the cooking liquid until the sauce thickens. Cook, stirring frequently, for 2–3 minutes. Season with pepper. Remove from the heat and keep warm.

To finish the dish, put the remaining olive oil in a large frying pan and warm over medium heat. Spread the drained cardoons in the pan and heat through gently for 8–10 minutes or until piping hot. Transfer to a warmed serving dish.

If necessary, reheat the sauce until simmering. Remove from the heat, stir in the cream, and adjust the seasonings. Pour the sauce over the cardoons, stir gently to coat, and serve soon.

Serves 6

Preparation 30 minutes
Cooking 45 minutes
3lb (1.3kg) small to medium
   cardoons
juice of 1 lemon
1 bouquet garni (see pp28–29)
3 tbsp olive oil
1 heaping tbsp flour
4 anchovy fillets packed in oil,
   drained and finely chopped
2 garlic cloves, crushed
fine sea salt and freshly ground
   black pepper to taste
3 tbsp light cream or half-and-half

"This recipe is an old Provençal winter classic. Cardoons can be quite tough and bitter, so make sure they aren't too big. Clean them carefully and rinse well in water with lemon juice."

Mesclun citronnette

The best place to make a salad dressing is in the bottom of the salad bowl. Stir the dressing ingredients well to combine, then put the leaves on top—but do not toss until you are ready to serve. Take care not to use too much dressing on delicate mixed baby leaves. They only need the lightest coating.

In the bottom of a salad bowl, mix together the lemon juice and mustard. Season with salt and pepper. Whisk in the oil and cream until well blended. Taste and adjust the seasonings.

Turn the mesclun leaves into the bowl. Just before serving, toss the leaves lightly but thoroughly with the sauce citronnette.

Variations

This tangy citrus dressing is very good with steamed or roasted vegetables—try it with zucchini, fennel, and leeks. Or use it to dress a salad of cooked fava beans and green beans.

The lemon juice can be replaced by freshly squeezed orange juice and 1 tsp of white wine vinegar. This is good with mesclun, soft lettuce, and lamb's lettuce.

Serves 4

Preparation 10 minutes
4 cups *mesclun* (mixed salad
  leaves), rinsed and dried

For the sauce citronnette
juice of ½ lemon
½ tsp Dijon mustard
fine sea salt and freshly ground
  black pepper to taste
5 tbsp olive oil
3 tbsp light cream or half-and-half

Always refresh salad leaves in plenty of very cold water before you dress them, even if they are dainty baby leaves that have already clearly been rinsed. Drain well and dry off in a salad spinner.

Salade d'échalotes aux pommes d'amour

This shallot and tomato dish is a sumptuous cooked salad—good in winter when tomatoes aren't at their flavorful best. Serve as an appetizer or to accompany pan-fried or grilled tuna steaks. It will keep for 1–2 days in the refrigerator.

Serves 6

Preparation 20 minutes
Cooking 40 minutes

6 fairly large, ripe tomatoes
fine sea salt and freshly ground
   black pepper to taste
6 tbsp olive oil
1½lb (675g) small shallots, peeled
2 cups dry white wine
2 cloves
15 black peppercorns
2 bay leaves
¼ cup sugar
1 sprig of fresh thyme
2 lemons
1 tbsp tomato paste
3 garlic cloves, crushed
leaves from 6 sprigs of
   flat-leaf parsley, chopped
leaves from 6 sprigs of fresh
   basil, chopped
¼ cup extra virgin olive oil

Bring a large saucepan of water to a boil. Cut a small cross through the skin on the base of each tomato, then immerse in the boiling water. Blanch large tomatoes for 1 minute, medium ones for 40 seconds. Remove with a slotted spoon and dip briefly in a bowl of ice water; then drain and peel away the skin. Cut the tomatoes in half, remove the seeds, then halve each half. Salt the tomatoes and drain in a colander.

Heat a sauté pan, add the olive oil, and cook the shallots over medium–low heat, stirring frequently, for 15 minutes or until softened but not browned.

Stir in the tomatoes and increase the heat to medium. Cook for 5 minutes, stirring occasionally. Add the white wine and continue cooking, still stirring from time to time, for 10 minutes longer, or until reduced and thickened.

Add the cloves, peppercorns, bay leaves, sugar, and thyme. Season lightly with salt and pepper. Stir in 1 cup of water and return to a boil.

Juice one of the lemons. Cut the second lemon into slices and cut each slice into quarters and discard the seeds. Add the lemon juice and pieces to the pan, then stir in the tomato paste and garlic. Let simmer over medium heat until reduced by more than half. Adjust the seasonings. Remove from the heat and set aside to cool.

Just before serving, stir in the chopped parsley, basil, and the extra virgin olive oil. Taste again and adjust the seasonings. Serve at room temperature or slightly chilled.

Take the skin from the tomatoes and gently squeeze out the seeds. Both skin and seeds would spoil the appearance of this colorful salad.

Salade niçoise

Salade niçoise has always been a flexible feast based on salad leaves, scallions, tomatoes, olives, olive oil, and anchovies. Flaked tuna and hard-boiled eggs are optional but desirable extras.

Serves 4

Preparation 30 minutes

1 large or 2 small lettuce heads of
   Boston or other leafy green
4 just ripe tomatoes
4 eggs, hard-boiled
3 large scallions (green onions)
8 anchovy fillets packed in oil
½ small red bell pepper
½lb (225g) cooked green beans
   (see p74)
2 tbsp small black olives
6oz (175g) canned tuna in olive
   oil, drained and flaked
2 tsp lemon juice

For the dressing

6 tbsp extra virgin olive oil
1 garlic clove, crushed
5 fresh basil leaves, finely
   chopped
1 tbsp red or white wine vinegar
fine sea salt and freshly ground
   black pepper to taste

To make the dressing, put all the ingredients in a cup and whisk well; then set aside to let the flavors blend while you prepare the salad.

Separate the lettuce leaves. Rinse, drain, and dry in a salad spinner. Tear the leaves into bite-size pieces. Halve the tomatoes, then cut each half into 2 or 3 wedges. Peel the eggs and quarter lengthwise. Chop both the white and green parts of the scallions. Drain the anchovy fillets well on paper towels, then cut each in half lengthwise. Remove seeds from the red pepper, then cut into thin strips.

Select a round or oval shallow bowl or platter. Put in some lettuce leaves, add a layer of tomato, and scatter in some green beans, red pepper, and scallion pieces. Repeat until you have used up all these ingredients.

Whisk the dressing again. Taste and adjust the seasonings. Spoon over the salad and toss gently.

To finish the salad, tuck in the hard-boiled eggs, scatter the olives on top, and distribute the anchovy and tuna flakes over the salad. Season with black pepper and sprinkle with the lemon juice. Serve soon.

"Avoid adding cooked potatoes, rice, or corn to your niçoise—they don't really fit into the mixture of fresh vegetables that makes up the original dish."

Frisée aux miettes de thon

Canned tuna is a great staple of the Provence pantry. Make sure the tuna is top quality and packed in olive oil. This simple salad makes a great little starter or main course for a light lunch.

Separate the lettuce leaves. Rinse, drain, and dry in a salad spinner. Put the tuna in a colander, shred with a fork, and let drain for a few minutes.

In the bottom of a large salad bowl, mix together the ingredients for the vinaigrette.

Toss the salad leaves in the dressing. Scatter the tuna flakes on top, toss again lightly, and sprinkle with the lemon juice just before serving.

Variation

A generous handful of purslane leaves makes a great addition to this salad. Simply rinse, drain, and toss with the lettuce and dressing.

Serves 4

Preparation 15 minutes
1 large head curly lettuce
6oz (175g) canned tuna in oil, drained
1 tbsp lemon juice

For the vinaigrette
¼ cup olive oil
1 tbsp white wine vinegar
½ tsp honey
2 tsp chopped fresh tarragon leaves
2 tsp chopped fresh basil leaves
fine sea salt and white pepper to taste

Salade de poivrons et tomates

This warm salad of peppers and tomatoes is redolent of summer—there's no need to add any garnish. It's great on its own, with slices of lightly toasted *pain de campagne* (country bread), or makes a splendid accompaniment to steamed new potatoes. It's also excellent reheated and stirred into Riz Pilaf (p292).

Preheat the oven to 400°F/200°C.

Halve the tomatoes. Sprinkle the cut sides with salt, then turn them cut side down on a baking sheet or in a colander and press down gently with the palm of your hand. Set aside to drain for 5 minutes.

Press the tomatoes again, then pour off the excess juices from the baking sheet. Turn the tomato halves cut side up. Drizzle with 1 tbsp olive oil and season lightly with salt and pepper. Place in the oven and roast for about 45 minutes.

Meanwhile, char and peel the peppers (see p65). Slice open, remove the seeds, and cut the flesh into strips. Put the pepper strips in the middle of a piece of foil and bring up the edges to make a loose parcel, sealing well. Place in the oven with the tomatoes and bake for 20 minutes.

When the tomatoes are cool enough to handle, skin them and cut into quarters. Place in a salad bowl.

Let the pepper strips cool down completely before adding them, with any juices, to the tomatoes.

Put the garlic in a cup. Spoon in the mustard and vinegar, season lightly, and mash together with a fork. Stir in the remaining oil. Adjust the seasonings.

Drizzle the dressing over the pepper and tomatoes. Stir again just before serving.

Serves 6

Preparation and cooking about 1¼ hours
6 large, ripe but firm vine-ripened tomatoes
fine sea salt and freshly ground black pepper to taste
6 tbsp olive oil, plus extra for greasing
4 ripe red bell peppers
2 garlic cloves, crushed
1 tsp Dijon mustard
1 tbsp red or white wine vinegar

Salt the tomatoes to draw out their juices. After draining, gently press them again to remove excess moisture.

Salade de tomates

This is the simplest of summer salads, but the tomatoes do need a little time to drain and then to blend flavors with the dressing, herbs, and shallots. It's the perfect choice for a warm, sunny day.

Serves 4

Preparation 15 minutes,
 plus draining and
 standing 30 minutes

6 very ripe, medium to large,
 vine-ripened tomatoes, cored

fine sea salt and freshly ground
 black pepper to taste

2 small shallots, very finely
 chopped

leaves from 4 sprigs of flat-leaf
 parsley, finely chopped

leaves from 2 sprigs of fresh
 basil, finely chopped

¼ cup extra virgin olive oil

2 tsp red or white wine vinegar

Cut the tomatoes into thin slices, put in a colander, and sprinkle lightly with salt. Let drain for 15–30 minutes, stirring from time to time.

Lift out the tomato slices, discarding some of the seeds and pulp. Arrange the slices in concentric circles on a round or oval platter. Scatter the shallots, chopped parsley, and basil over the top.

In a cup, whisk together the olive oil and vinegar. Season lightly with salt and pepper. Drizzle this dressing over the salad, then let stand at room temperature for 10–30 minutes. Serve with chunks of fresh bread to mop up the juices.

"You need to use good, just ripe tomatoes and plenty of fragrant fresh herbs when you prepare this salad. It's just not worth making with bland ingredients."

Salade de pois chiches

This warm, substantial chickpea salad was traditionally served in Provence on Palm Sunday, the week before Easter. Superstition had it that it prevented warts and skin diseases for the rest of the year...

Rinse and drain the chickpeas, then put them in a large saucepan with plenty of fresh cold water. Add the baking soda and a little salt. Bring to a boil and simmer for 15 minutes. Drain and rinse.

Rinse the pan, then return the chickpeas and cover with plenty of boiling water. Cook for 40–50 minutes or until just tender. Drain.

While the chickpeas are cooking, mix together all the ingredients for the dressing in a salad bowl. Blanch and skin the tomatoes (see p90); remove the seeds and dice the flesh.

Drain the chickpeas and turn into the salad bowl. Toss to coat with the dressing, then stir in the diced tomatoes. Adjust the seasonings. Serve barely warm.

Variations

A spoonful of *poutargue* (salted and pressed grey mullet roe) is an optional extra. You can also stir in a handful of rocket (arugula), baby spinach, or dandelion leaves at the last minute. Blanched wild or thin green asparagus also makes a good addition.

Serves 4

Preparation 15 minutes, plus overnight soaking
Cooking about 1½ hours, plus cooling at least 30 minutes

8oz (225g) dried chickpeas (garbanzo beans), soaked overnight in lightly salted cold water
1 scant tsp baking soda
2 medium tomatoes

For the dressing
¼ cup olive oil
2 small garlic cloves, crushed
1½ tsp Dijon mustard
yolk of 1 large hard-boiled egg, chopped
2 small scallions (green onions), finely chopped
leaves from 1 sprig of fresh thyme, or 1 tsp dried thyme
leaves from 2 sprigs of flat-leaf parsley, finely chopped
12 fresh chives, finely chopped
fine sea salt and freshly ground black pepper to taste

dinner

Menu

soupe aux
fèves fraîches

—

gigotines de poulet
farcies à la sariette

salade verte
à l'huile de basilic

—

tian de pommes

Soupe aux fèves fraîches

Baby fava bean soup is a perfect spring starter. Try serving it topped with croûtons and a splash of extra virgin olive oil. If you take the trouble to press it through a sieve after blending, you'll have an exquisite, elegant soup—worth the effort for a special meal.

To make the croûtons, cut the bread into ½in (1.5cm) cubes. Heat the oil in a large frying pan over medium-high heat. Add the bread cubes, spreading them out. Cook for a minute, then stir to turn them over. Fry for another minute. Spread the croûtons over a large plate lined with paper towels. Pat with more paper towels to absorb excess oil. Set aside.

In a large soup pot or flameproof casserole, heat the oil over medium heat. Add the onions and leek. Cook, stirring frequently, for 10 minutes, or until softened but not browned.

Meanwhile, shell the fava beans. Add to the pot with the garlic, chives, and potatoes. Stir, then pour in about 10½ cups water. Season lightly with salt and pepper and stir in the radish leaves. Turn up the heat a little and bring to a boil, then reduce heat and let bubble gently for 15–20 minutes.

Let cool a little, then press through a food mill. Alternatively, working in batches, process briefly in a food processor or blender, then press through a sieve. (If you prefer a more rustic soup, omit the sieving, in which case the soup will serve 6–8 people.) Reheat until piping hot before serving, topped with the croûtons.

Serves 4-6

Preparation 20 minutes
Cooking about 1 hour
3 tbsp olive oil
3 large mild onions, sliced
1 leek, sliced
3lb (1.3kg) fava beans
4 garlic cloves, crushed
a small handful of fresh chives, chopped
4 new potatoes, peeled and chopped
fine sea salt and freshly ground black pepper to taste
leaves from a bunch of fresh radishes, well washed

For the fried croûtons
3 slices bread
3 tbsp olive oil

Quickly fry cubes of bread in hot olive oil to make crisp little croûtons to scatter over the soup.

Gigotines de poulet farcies à la sarriette

The word *gigotine* is used to describe a partially-boned and stuffed chicken leg that ends up looking like a mini *gigot*, a French-trimmed leg of lamb. Summer savory gives this dish its distinctive flavor—similar to thyme, but with a bit more bite.

Serves 4

Preparation 20 minutes
Cooking 1½ hours

4 leg-thigh portions of chicken,
   with thigh bones removed, or
   4 large boneless chicken thighs
fine sea salt and freshly ground
   black pepper to taste
1 skinless, boneless chicken breast
3 tbsp peanut oil
white of 1 leek, finely chopped
3 small shallots, finely chopped
2 garlic cloves, thinly sliced
leaves from 2 sprigs of fresh
   thyme, or 1 tsp dried thyme
6 fresh summer savory leaves,
   or 1 tsp dried savory
1 small egg
½ tsp grated fresh nutmeg
unsalted butter for greasing
1 celery rib, chopped
1 carrot, chopped
1 large mild onion, chopped

Season the chicken legs inside and out with salt and pepper. Cover and refrigerate for at least 15–20 minutes, or longer if convenient.

Finely dice the chicken breast. In a large sauté pan, heat the oil over medium heat. Add the diced chicken and cook until lightly browned. Add the leek, shallots, and garlic. Cook for 10–15 minutes, stirring frequently. Stir in the thyme and savory. Remove from the heat and let cool for 5 minutes. Stir in the egg and nutmeg. Season lightly with salt and pepper and mix well.

Preheat the oven to 400°F/200°C. Butter a large, deep gratin dish.

Using a tablespoon, spread the stuffing mixture over the insides of the chicken legs. Fold to enclose and secure with wooden toothpicks. Place the stuffed legs in the buttered dish seam-side down. Scatter the celery, carrot, and onion over the top. Drizzle with 1 cup of water. Cover with foil and bake for 50 minutes.

Take the dish out of the oven, remove the foil, and stir. Return the dish to the oven, uncovered, to cook 20 minutes longer.

Lift out the chicken and put on a hot serving dish. Keep warm. Pour the cooking liquid and vegetables into a saucepan and bring to a boil over high heat. Let boil briskly until the liquid is reduced by one-third. Push the mixture through a chinois or fine sieve directly onto the chicken. Serve at once.

Put only enough stuffing in the chicken legs to replace the bone, so you can close them neatly and press into the original shape.

Salade verte à l'huile de basilic

Soft baby leaves have a tender sweetness that goes well with the mildly peppery flavor of radicchio and this basil oil salad dressing.

Serves 4

Preparation 15 minutes

1 small head soft lettuce, or 1 small
   head radicchio
3 cups mixed soft baby
   salad leaves
½ garlic clove
¼ cup basil-infused olive oil
   (see below)
2 tsp red wine vinegar
fine sea salt and freshly ground
   black pepper to taste
leaves from 2 sprigs of
   flat-leaf parsley
a few fresh chives

Separate the lettuce and radicchio leaves and tear into bite-size pieces. Rinse all the salad leaves, then drain and dry in a salad spinner.

Rub the salad bowl with the cut side of the garlic, then discard the garlic. Put the oil and vinegar in the bowl, season with salt and pepper, and stir to blend. Add the salad leaves.

Finely chop together the parsley and chives, and scatter over the leaves.

Just before serving, toss the salad. Taste and adjust the seasonings, then serve.

Huile parfumé au basilic

Blanch a generous handful of fresh basil leaves in boiling water for 1–2 minutes, adding 1–2 unpeeled garlic cloves for added flavor, if you like. Drain in a sieve and refresh under cold running water. Pat dry. Peel the garlic if using. Put ⅔ cup olive oil in a saucepan and heat until almost bubbling hot. Remove from the heat and stir in the basil and the garlic (if using). Let cool. When cool, strain the oil into a clean bottle and discard the basil leaves and garlic. Use at once, or refrigerate, covered. Return to room temperature before using.

You can use the same technique to infuse oil with herbs other than basil, such as fresh rosemary, thyme, oregano, or marjoram.

Tian de pommes

This apple gratin is an old family recipe, handed down to Gui Gedda by his grandfather. You don't need to peel the apples as long as they are thin skinned. In fact, the slices look very appetizing with their rosy pink seams.

Preheat the oven to 400°F/200°C.

Core the unpeeled apples using a knife or apple corer, if you have one. Cut the apples in half, then slice into thin wedges.

In a large non-stick frying pan, melt the butter over medium–high heat. Gently stir in the apples and cook for 3–5 minutes or until lightly browned but not soft. Remove from the heat and set aside.

In a large bowl, whisk together the milk, cream, almonds, and cornstarch. Add the eggs and sugar. Whisk again vigorously until well blended. Turn the apples into the mixture and stir gently with a wooden spoon.

Lightly butter a *tian* or gratin dish or an ovenproof frying pan. Spread the apple batter in the dish or pan and place in the oven.

Bake for 45–50 minutes or until the batter is set and golden. Sprinkle with confectioners' sugar, if you like, and serve hot or warm, directly from the dish.

Serves 4

Preparation 15 minutes
Cooking about 1 hour
6 crisp, juicy eating apples
5 tbsp unsalted butter, plus extra
  for greasing
½ cup cold milk
1 cup cold light cream or
  half-and-half
1 cup ground almonds
1 tbsp cornstarch
4 eggs
¼ cup sugar
sifted confectioners' (powdered)
  sugar (optional)

Core the apples whole ... then it will be easy to cut them into neat segments and the flesh won't discolor as much.

wednesday

On the menu today
is an olive oil sampling to get your
tastebuds going. Learn how to make
the classic sauces of Provence,
and how best to use and serve
them. Find out just how easy it is
to make mouthwatering, vibrantly
flavored omelettes. Prepare a
splendid three-course dinner with
a sensational sweet ending.

Olives et huile d'olive

Olives and olive oil are as much a part of the pleasures of Provençal eating as the ancient olive groves are part of the Mediterranean landscape. Just like the fruit of the vine, the fruits of the olive tree are the products of the environment—the soil, the location, and the climate all give olives and olive oils their unique characteristics.

Popular eating varieties of olives are fleshy black Tanches from the Nyons area in the north of Provence. The olive of Nice is Cailletier, small, black, and wrinkly looking—often used in salade niçoise and pissaladière. Violette, with purpley hues, has a firm, plump texture.

Pitting olives requires patience and a sharp, narrow knife. Hold the olive in one hand, cut into the olive, and gently ease your knife around the pit to loosen and remove it.

All olives are green if you pick them unripe—they turn black if you leave them to ripen. If you bite into an olive straight off the tree, whether green or black, its unpleasantly bitter taste will make your mouth pucker. Curing olives with salt or oil and herbs soon turns them into versatile ingredients and the perfect easy nibble to serve with a glass of chilled wine.

Olive oil

A golden drizzle on roasted vegetables, an irresistible salad dressing, the simplest dip for crusty fresh bread… the extra virgin olive oil of Provence has myriad uses and adds magic to everyday foods. Fresh is best: unlike good wine, olive oil never improves with age.

Compared to Italy and Spain, Provence's production of extra virgin olive oil is modest, but the oils it produces are of a very high standard. Extra virgin olive oil is simply pressed from the crushed flesh and pits of just-picked olives in a process that hasn't changed much in hundreds of years.

The best way to taste an extra virgin oil is to treat it like a fine wine. First, enjoy the color. Many Provence oils look bright and shine like gold. A green, cloudy color means the oil hasn't been filtered.

Pour a little oil into a white ramekin. Cut fresh bread into small chunks. Dip a piece of bread into the oil. Take a sniff. What is the aroma like?

The next step is to taste. Think of words like delicate, fruity with a strong olive flavor, sweet, rustic. Then savor the finish— it might be peppery, spicy, or just a little bitter.

Always buy the freshest olive oil available. Once opened, a bottle should be kept in a cool, dark place and used within a few months. After 3 months the fruity freshness of extra virgin olive oil will have disappeared.

Extra virgin olive oil is far too fragile for cooking. Use standard olive oil instead and save precious extra virgin olive oil for the finishing touch to a dish.

Bagna cauda

To serve with this warm anchovy and garlic dip, you will want a variety of at least five different vegetables—about 1½lb (650g) total weight for 6 people. To eat, dip the vegetables into the hot sauce. In your other hand, hold a slice of bread to catch the delicious drips—save eating the sauce-soaked bread for the end.

Boil or steam the potatoes until just tender; drain. Peel the beet and cut into wedges or thick matchsticks. Trim the artichokes (see p146) and quarter lengthwise. Cut the fennel, carrot, and celery into matchsticks, and the cauliflower into florets. Separate the chicory and cabbage leaves. Arrange all of the selected vegetables on a platter.

About 10 minutes before serving, start the bagna cauda. Melt the butter, add the anchovies and garlic, and season with pepper. Stir and mash with a fork and spoon to dissolve the anchovies in the hot butter. Pour in the milk and light cream, and cook over moderate heat for 5 minutes, stirring, without letting the sauce boil.

Put the pot of sauce on a stand above a plate warmer or on a hot plate to keep warm. Surround with the vegetables and bread, letting guests help themselves.

Bagna cauda à l'ancienne

For a stronger-flavored dip, melt the anchovies and garlic in ¾ cup olive oil—milk and light cream make the sauce a little milder but are less typical of authentic old-fashioned Provence cooking.

Make the bagna cauda in the pan in which it will be served, such as an attractive enameled saucepan, a flameproof cheese fondue pot, or the top of a bain marie.

Serves 6

Preparation and cooking
30 minutes

Select from the following:
  1lb (450g) baby new potatoes, scrubbed; 1 cooked beet;
  3 tender baby artichokes;
  1 fennel bulb; 1 carrot; 1 small head celery; ½ small cauliflower;
  1 head chicory or curly endive; tender inner leaves from 1 curly green cabbage; 1 bunch of radishes, trimmed; 8oz (225g) cherry tomatoes
6 thick slices of French bread
For the bagna cauda
8oz (2 sticks) unsalted butter
30 anchovy fillets in oil or salt, drained, or rinsed and drained
cloves from 1 large head garlic, thinly sliced
freshly ground black pepper
¼ cup milk
½ cup light cream or half-and-half

Anchoïade

Serve this savory anchovy paste with baked croûtons, or as a snack with a glass of chilled dry rosé. Anchoïade is also a wonderful flavor-enhancer smeared over grilled fish, beef, veal, and pork.

Serves 4

Preparation 20 minutes

12 anchovy fillets in oil, drained
2 garlic cloves, smashed
6 tbsp extra virgin olive oil
1 tsp red wine vinegar
¼ tsp Dijon mustard
2 tbsp finely chopped
  flat-leaf parsley
freshly ground black pepper
  to taste
baked croûtons to serve
  (see p118)

Put the anchovies and garlic in a bowl and add 1 tbsp olive oil. Using two forks, mash together to make a paste.

Still using the forks or, if you feel more comfortable, a small whisk, beat in the rest of the oil, 1 tbsp at a time.

Stir in the vinegar, mustard, and parsley, and season with pepper. You should have a thick, coarse purée. If not serving at once, cover and refrigerate.

"A little anchoïade goes a long way. Just a teaspoon stirred into a sauce or soup adds a distinct but subtle Provençal magic."

Tapenade

Tapenade, Provence's most famous pantry sauce, comes from the Provençal word for capers, *tapeno*. Everybody thinks of it as an olive dip, but it is in fact a caper sauce. Garlic is an optional extra—add a little, if you wish. Tapenade has many uses, not just as an appetizer.

Put all the ingredients except the olive oil and pepper in the bowl of a blender or food processor. Process briefly until you have a coarse purée.

With the motor running, add the olive oil in a slow, steady stream to make a thick paste. Season with pepper. If not using at once, put the tapenade in a small jar or bowl and cover with a layer of olive oil. Refrigerate, and use within 3–5 days.

Tapenade verte

Use pitted green olives instead of black olives, and add the grated zest and juice of the remaining ½ lemon.

Tapenade au basilic

Add 4–6 chopped fresh basil leaves to the ingredients for green tapenade.

Tapenade à l'aubergine

For a milder dip, add the baked flesh of a small eggplant (see p63) to the ingredients for tapenade or green tapenade.

Tapenade au thon

Drain a small can of tuna (about 3oz—or half of a 6oz can) and add to the ingredients for tapenade or green tapenade.

Serves 4-6

Preparation 15 minutes
7oz (200g), or about 1¼ cups
  black olives, pitted
3 tbsp capers, drained and rinsed
finely grated zest and juice
  of ½ lemon
1 anchovy fillet in oil, drained
5 tbsp extra virgin olive oil
freshly ground black pepper
  to taste

Rouille

Spread this red, hot pepper and saffron mayonnaise over baked croûtons or serve with Soupe de Poissons (p269). Rouille can be kept for a couple of days, covered and refrigerated, but it might need whisking briefly to re-emulsify.

Serves 4-6

Preparation 20 minutes
3 garlic cloves, smashed
coarse sea salt
freshly ground black pepper
  to taste
small pinch of saffron strands
½ tsp cayenne pepper
½ tsp paprika
2 medium egg yolks
1 cup olive oil

For the baked croûtons
1 small day-old baguette

Using a pestle and mortar, pound the garlic with 1 tsp coarse sea salt. Season with pepper, then add the saffron, cayenne, paprika, and egg yolks. Pound all the ingredients together. Once you have a smooth mixture, let it rest for 5 minutes.

Gradually beat in the oil, a few drops at a time, as if making mayonnaise. Once the sauce has thickened and emulsified, start adding the oil in a slow trickle, beating constantly. Taste and adjust the seasoning. Cover and refrigerate for 30 minutes.

Preheat the oven to 400°F/200°C. Thinly slice the baguette. Put the slices on a baking sheet and toast in the oven for 4–5 minutes until crisp.

Put the rouille in a small bowl and let guests dip the croûtons into it. Alternatively, spread the rouille over the toasts and arrange on a tray or platter.

Rouille à la tomate

Add 1 tsp tomato paste before you start adding the oil.

Rouille au basilic

Add 1 tbsp finely chopped fresh basil leaves before the oil, then stir in another tablespoon of basil just before serving.

Your rouille should be very solid at the end—ideally firm enough for the pestle to stand upright in the mortar.

Rouille au corail d'oursin

Paprika gives a beautiful red color to this very French mayonnaise, and sea urchin coral adds a superb flavor. You can replace the sea urchin coral with the livers of 2 red mullets or rascasses.

Using a pestle and mortar, pound the garlic with 1 tsp of coarse sea salt. Season with pepper, then add the paprika, half the coral, and the potato. Pound all the ingredients together thoroughly to form a paste.

Add the egg yolks and continue pounding vigorously. Once you have a smooth mixture, let rest for 5 minutes.

Gradually beat in the oil, a few drops at a time, as for making mayonnaise. Once the sauce has thickened and emulsified, you can start adding the oil in a slow trickle, still beating constantly. Stir in the rest of the coral. Taste and adjust the seasoning before serving with baked croûtons.

Serves 4-6

Preparation 20 minutes
2 garlic cloves, smashed
coarse sea salt
freshly ground black pepper
  to taste
1 tsp paprika
coral from 12 sea urchins
½ boiled potato, peeled
2 medium egg yolks
1 cup olive oil
baked croûtons to serve
  (see p118)

"The fragile spikes of sea urchins make them difficult to handle. Take great care, protect your hands with thick gloves or a thick towel, and cut off the tops with scissors without applying too much pressure. Scoop out the coral—it looks like small orange petals—with a teaspoon and enjoy its delicately briny taste."

Ketchup à la provençale

A Provençal tomato ketchup? Why not? There are plenty of luscious, vine-ripened tomatoes in Provence, and they make a lovely summer sauce for barbecued meats and to serve with omelettes.

Put the tomatoes, onions, and olive oil in a large, heavy saucepan or Dutch oven and stir well. Cover and cook over medium heat for 30–40 minutes, stirring frequently.

Set aside to cool a little, then pulse in a food processor or blender until coarsely puréed. Return to the pan. Add ¼ cup water, the sugar, and vinegar. Cook uncovered over low heat for 30 minutes, stirring a few times.

Remove from the heat. Stir in the remaining ingredients. Let cool for a few minutes, then press through a fine sieve into a bowl. Set aside to cool to room temperature.

When the ketchup is cool, spoon into a clean jar or small bottles. Store in the refrigerator for up to 1 month.

Serves 6

Preparation 15 minutes, plus cooling
Cooking 1½ hours
3lb (1.3kg) tomatoes, cut into quarters
2lb (900g) mild onions, thinly sliced
¼ cup olive oil
⅓ cup sugar
½ cup red wine vinegar
1 heaping tsp fine sea salt
1 tbsp Dijon mustard
½ tsp grated fresh nutmeg
1 tsp paprika
½ tsp cayenne pepper
½ tsp dried thyme
1 tsp ground ginger

Stew juicy tomatoes with onions until broken down to a pulp, then sieve to create a velvety smooth, richly flavored sauce.

Coulis à la tomate

The simplest of tomato sauces. It's hard to improve upon the flavor of genuine sun-ripened summer tomatoes, but you can add a very modest amount of fresh basil, a touch of oregano, or even tarragon to the blender or food processor.

Serves 6

Preparation 10 minutes
Cooking 20 minutes
1½ tbsp unsalted butter
1½ tbsp olive oil
2lb (900g) ripe tomatoes, coarsely chopped
fine sea salt and freshly ground black pepper to taste

Melt the butter in a large sauté pan over medium heat. Add the olive oil, then add the tomatoes. Increase the heat to high and cook for 5 minutes, stirring occasionally.

Reduce the heat to low, partially cover the pan, and cook for 15 minutes longer. Remove from the heat and set aside to cool.

Season with salt and pepper. Working in batches if necessary, scrape the tomatoes into a blender or food processor. Process to a coarse purée, then push through a sieve into a bowl. Discard the seeds and pulp. Adjust the seasonings. Use at once, or cover and refrigerate for up to 5 days, or freeze for up to 3 months.

"In winter, throw a teaspoon of sugar into the pan with the tomatoes, to make them sweeter."

Sauce tomate classique

Traditional tomato sauce simmers slowly until thick and fragrant. More full bodied than the coulis on the opposite page, it includes some diced bacon (lardons), preferably smoked for extra flavor. Just like the coulis, this sauce freezes well and is worth having on hand to dress pasta and add to casseroles.

Place a sauté pan over medium heat. Add the olive oil, then the onions and lardons. Cook, stirring, for 5 minutes.

Add the chopped tomatoes and garlic, sugar, parsley, thyme, and oregano. Season lightly with salt and pepper and add 1 cup hot water. Cook uncovered over medium heat for 30 minutes, stirring frequently.

Let cool until just warm. Working in batches if necessary, spoon the mixture into a blender or food processor and process to a coarse purée.

Push through a sieve, pressing down well with the back of a spoon or a pestle to extract as much sauce as possible. Drizzle ½ cup of lukewarm water into the sieve at the end and continue pushing.

Adjust the seasonings. Reheat the sauce before serving.

Serves 6

Preparation 10 minutes
Cooking 30 minutes

5 tbsp olive oil
2 mild onions, finely chopped
¼lb (115g) lardons (bacon cut into ½in dice)
2lb (900g) tomatoes, chopped
6 garlic cloves, crushed
1 tsp sugar
2 tbsp chopped flat-leaf parsley
2 sprigs each of fresh thyme and oregano
fine sea salt and freshly ground black pepper to taste

Persillade

More of a salsa than a sauce because it requires no cooking, this robust-tasting condiment is a great accompaniment to cold cuts, poached meat and fish, and stews. It's also excellent stirred into steamed or boiled new potatoes, plain green lentils, or chickpeas (garbanzo beans).

Serves 4-6

Preparation 10 minutes
leaves from 6 sprigs of
  flat-leaf parsley
3 garlic cloves, smashed
coarse sea salt
freshly ground black pepper
  to taste
3–4 tbsp extra virgin olive oil
  (optional)

Put the parsley and garlic on a chopping board. Sprinkle with ½ tsp of coarse sea salt. Using a mezzaluna or a chopping knife you feel comfortable with, chop very finely. Season with pepper and mix well.

To use as a topping, simply scatter the mixture over the dish of your choice. To use as a paste or sauce, stir in the olive oil.

Variations
To give a citrus tang to a *persillade* topping, add 1 tsp finely grated orange or lemon zest.

To make a splendid but simple sauce for pasta, try adding a mashed anchovy fillet to a *persillade* paste.

"If there's a choice, take a tip from Provençal cooks and always use flat-leaf parsley rather than the curly variety. Its flavor is at the same time more pronounced and less assertive. You'll also find it easier to chop than curly parsley."

Sauce verte

Chopped fresh herbs give this green mayonnaise-style sauce a vibrant freshness and zing. To make it a bit more savory you can add a drained anchovy fillet at the same time as the garlic. Serve the sauce with cold meat, poached chicken or fish, or asparagus.

Put the egg yolk, mustard, and a little salt in the bowl of a blender or food processor. Add the garlic and pulse on and off a few times. With the motor running, drizzle the peanut oil very slowly through the feed tube. Once the mixture becomes thick and creamy, you can add the oil a little faster. Process in half the herbs, then pour in the olive oil in a slow, steady stream through the feed tube.

Add the lemon juice and the remaining herbs. Taste and adjust the seasonings. Let sit for 5 minutes.

Your sauce should look very thick and solid. If you like, thin it down with 1–2 tbsp warm water or cream. Sauce verte can be refrigerated, covered, for up to 48 hours.

Serves 4-6

Preparation 15 minutes

1 large egg yolk
2 tsp Dijon mustard
fine sea salt and freshly ground black pepper to taste
1 small garlic clove, crushed
⅔ cup peanut oil
2 tsp finely chopped flat-leaf parsley
2 tsp finely chopped fresh basil
1 tsp finely chopped fresh tarragon leaves or dill weed
½ tsp fresh marjoram or oregano leaves
½ cup olive oil
1 tbsp lemon juice
1–2 tbsp warm water, or 1 tbsp light cream or half-and-half (optional)

Aïoli complet

This dish is traditionally served on an oval platter with the bowl of garlicky sauce, called *aïoli*, in the center. Let your guests shell their own eggs and peel their potatoes, if desired. You can use other vegetables such as sweet potatoes, asparagus spears, fennel, salsify, or *bâtons* of celery root. Poached salt cod (see p151) is another traditional ingredient.

First prepare the sauce. Using a pestle and mortar, pound the garlic with a small pinch of salt. Season with pepper and add the egg yolks. Stir and pound for about 2 minutes to make a thick, coarse paste, then let sit for 5 minutes.

Gradually beat in the oil, a few drops at a time, as for making mayonnaise. After a few minutes, once the sauce becomes thick and creamy, drizzle in the oil slowly, still beating constantly with the pestle, always in the same direction. Aïoli must have a very thick texture—the pestle should stand up by itself in the bowl. Cover and keep in a cool place or the refrigerator while you prepare the vegetables.

Peel or scrape the carrots. Trim the green beans. Trim the cauliflower or broccoli, then cut into florets. Cook the vegetables separately in pots of boiling salted water. Cook the unpeeled potatoes until just done, then drain. Cook the carrots until just tender, then drain. Cook the green beans until just tender, then drain and refresh under cold running water. Cook the cauliflower or broccoli florets for 3–5 minutes until barely cooked—they should still be a little crunchy (the broccoli will cook faster than the cauliflower). Drain and refresh under cold running water.

Meanwhile, boil the eggs for 9 minutes. Drain and refresh, but leave in the shell.

Arrange all the prepared vegetables and the eggs on a platter and serve barely warm, with the aïoli sauce.

Serves 4

Preparation 30 minutes
Cooking 30 minutes
12–16 small carrots
1lb (450g) green beans
1 small cauliflower, or 1 head
  broccoli, about ½lb (225g)
4 medium boiling potatoes
4 medium eggs

For the aïoli sauce
4 garlic cloves, smashed
fine sea salt and freshly ground
  black pepper to taste
2 medium egg yolks
1 cup olive oil

You cannot hurry an aïoli, so be patient. Allow the egg yolks time to settle after you've worked them in, and add the oil drop by drop until the sauce gels together.

Beurre persillé

Savory butters (*beurres composés*) are usually a simple combination of unsalted butter and fresh herbs, and can be made in minutes, then chilled or frozen. If you want a more intense garlic flavor in this parsley butter—particularly if you are making it to stuff mushrooms or to smear over mussels or clams before grilling—you can use extra garlic.

Makes about ¾ cup

Preparation 15 minutes
1 shallot, chopped
3 tbsp chopped flat-leaf parsley
1–2 garlic cloves, crushed
1 tsp drained capers
1 tsp lemon juice
11 tbsp (5½oz) soft unsalted
    butter, cut into pieces
fine sea salt and freshly ground
    black pepper to taste

Put the shallot, parsley, garlic, and capers in a food processor (preferably one with a small bowl). Pulse the machine on and off quickly to a form a coarse paste, then scrape down the sides of the bowl with a spatula. Add the lemon juice and butter, and process to blend. Taste and season with salt and pepper.

Cover and refrigerate for at least 1 hour before using. Alternatively, shape the butter into a cylinder, wrap tightly in plastic wrap, and refrigerate for up to 2 weeks, or freeze for up to 2 months.

Variations
Follow the same method to prepare tarragon, dill, basil, or chive butter, replacing the parsley with these herbs, but omit the shallot and capers.

Beurre d'anchois
Add 1–2 drained and chopped oil-packed anchovy fillets to the food processor at the beginning of the recipe. Be sure to taste before adding salt to the recipe.

"If you shape your savory butter into a cylinder, you can just slice off discs as needed and use it to melt on vegetables, fish, or meat to add a genuine touch of Provence flavor to your cooking."

Beurre aux herbes de Provence

Warming the herbs with a little garlic first helps to release their aromatic and sometimes mildly resinous flavors. This flavored butter is made with a mixture of herbs, but with their distinctive strong flavors, individual Mediterranean herbs can also be used on their own.

Heat the oil and 2 tsp of the butter in a small frying pan. Add the herbs and garlic, and cook over a low heat, stirring, for 1–2 minutes. Drain on paper towels.

Transfer the herbs and garlic to a food processor (preferably one with a small bowl) or a bowl and mix in the rest of the soft butter, using two forks in the bowl. Season lightly with salt and more generously with pepper.

Cover and refrigerate for at least 1 hour before using. Alternatively, shape the butter into a cylinder, wrap tightly in plastic wrap, and refrigerate for up to 2 weeks, or freeze for up to 2 months.

Variation

For another Provençal herb butter, replace the herbs listed above with 1 tsp marjoram leaves, 2 tsp finely chopped rosemary, and 2 tsp finely chopped summer savory.

Beurre à la sauge

Use 5 tsp finely chopped fresh sage instead of the herbs listed above. This is excellent with zucchini, pumpkin, grilled or pan-fried veal, and many rice dishes.

Makes about ⅔ cup

Preparation 15 minutes
Cooking 5 minutes

2 tsp peanut oil
7 tbsp (3½oz) soft unsalted butter
1 tsp fresh oregano leaves, finely chopped
2 tsp fresh thyme leaves
2 tsp finely chopped fresh rosemary
1 garlic clove, crushed
fine sea salt and freshly ground black pepper to taste

Sauce mousseline au caramel de miel

Creamy honey caramel sauce makes a very versatile accompaniment for cakes and fruit desserts. If you are new to caramel-making, you'll find honey less intimidating than sugar. But it's still important to keep an eye on the mixture from the moment it starts to bubble.

Serves 8

Preparation and cooking
  20 minutes, plus cooling
½ cup liquid honey
2 cups single cream or half-and-
  half, chilled

Put the honey in a small, heavy saucepan. Warm over medium heat until bubbling gently. Cook until the honey begins to turn a little darker.

Meanwhile, in another small, heavy saucepan, warm half of the cream without letting it boil. As soon as the honey has darkened, remove from the heat and whisk in the hot cream. Let cool to room temperature, stirring from time to time.

Whisk the rest of the chilled cream in a bowl until light and airy. Whisk the cream into the cold caramel sauce to make it thick and fluffy. Cover and chill until needed, but use the sauce on the same day it is made. Before serving, lightly whisk the sauce again if it has separated.

Sauce mousseline au caramel

Honey caramel is a favorite, but you can replace it with a sugar caramel. Put ½ cup sugar in a small heavy pan with 3 tbsp water. Melt the sugar over medium heat, stirring occasionally. Stop stirring and let the mixture bubble gently until the caramel turns golden. Take the pan off the heat immediately and add the warmed cream as described above, followed by the whisked cream.

Closely watch the simmering honey and take it off the heat the moment it begins to turn darker. Immediately start whisking in the hot cream to stop the cooking process.

Coulis de framboises

Sweet, smooth fruit coulis, or sauces, such as this one made with raspberries, are very good with meringues, ice creams, and many cakes. Coulis can be stored in the refrigerator for 3-4 days or frozen for up to 2 months.

Serves 6-8

Preparation 10 minutes
Cooking 5 minutes

1lb (450g) fresh raspberries or
  frozen unsweetened raspberries
3–4 tbsp sugar
1 tbsp grated orange zest
1 tbsp lemon juice

Combine the raspberries, sugar, and orange zest in a saucepan. Bring to a boil over high heat, stirring constantly.

Reduce the heat to medium and cook for 3 minutes, stirring and mashing the raspberries. Remove from the heat and let cool 5–10 minutes.

Push through a fine sieve into a bowl, pressing down well with the back of the spoon to squeeze out as much pulp as possible. Also use the spoon to scrape off the raspberry pulp sticking to the underside of the sieve. Stir the lemon juice into the sauce. Cover and refrigerate until needed.

Variations
Use the same method to prepare fresh apricot coulis (the apricots will need to simmer for 10 minutes), or peach or plum coulis.

Compote de figues

Serve this delicious fresh fig preserve with vanilla ice cream, yogurt, or fresh cream cheese. It can be kept in the refrigerator for up to 2 weeks.

Rinse, trim, and chop the figs. Slice the lemon and orange halves very thinly. Put the figs and citrus slices in a large bowl with the sugar and ½ cup water. Stir, then cover and refrigerate for 24 hours.

Turn the contents of the bowl into a heavy saucepan. Place over medium heat, cover, and bring to a simmer. Let the mixture bubble gently for 50 minutes, with the pan partly covered, stirring occasionally.

Remove from the heat and let cool for 30 minutes. Meanwhile, thoroughly rinse two 1 pint jars with boiling water; drain.

Spoon the warm preserve into the jars and let cool, then cover tightly. Use at once, or refrigerate.

Serves 8

Preparation 10 minutes,
  plus macerating 24 hours
Cooking 1 hour
2lb (900g) fresh figs
½ lemon, seeded
½ orange, seeded
3½ cups sugar

Salade de figues

If you like, you can make a quick version of this preserve into a cooked fruit salad. Simply reduce the cooking time to 8 minutes, then let cool. Serve at room temperature within 12 hours, or refrigerate and use within 48 hours.

"Cooked fruit salads are just as good as an easy-to-digest way to end a meal as they are at breakfast to start the day. Try cooking plums and apricots in the same way as the figs."

Omelette aux cébettes

A simple but delicious flat omelette, this is a lovely way to make the most of the mild flavor of the green tops of scallions. The omelette is perfect for a springtime lunch.

Cut the scallions into thin slices. Heat 2 tsp of the oil in a non-stick 9–10in (22–25cm) omelette pan. Spread the scallion slices in the pan and cook over medium heat, stirring, until softened. Drain in a colander or sieve, then turn into a small bowl.

Break the eggs into another bowl, season lightly, and whisk to mix the yolks and whites. Add the scallions. Let sit for 30 minutes to blend flavors.

Wipe the omelette pan clean with a paper towel. Return to medium–high heat and add the remaining 2½ tsp of oil.

Lightly whisk the egg mixture. Pour into the pan and cook, tilting the pan over the heat to enable the eggs to spread out as they cook. Once the omelette is set, swirl the butter over the surface to make it shine. Serve at once, cut into wedges.

Serves 2

Preparation 10 minutes, plus resting 30 minutes
Cooking 5 minutes

green parts of 6 scallions (green onions)
1½ tbsp peanut oil
6 medium eggs
fine sea salt and freshly ground black pepper to taste
1½ tbsp unsalted butter

Turn the cooked scallions into the eggs and whisk briefly. Let sit so the onions can delicately flavor the eggs.

Frittata aux pommes de terre

This flat omelette with potatoes and garlic is substantial enough to serve as a main course with a leafy green salad on the side. Chopped cooked artichoke bottoms can be used instead of potatoes, if you prefer.

Serves 2-3

Preparation 10 minutes
Cooking 5 minutes

4 small new potatoes
2 tbsp olive oil
1 scallion (green onion), chopped
1 garlic clove, crushed
1 tbsp finely chopped
　flat-leaf parsley
6 medium eggs
fine sea salt and freshly ground
　black pepper to taste
1½ tbsp unsalted butter

Cook the potatoes in boiling salted water until tender, then drain. When cool enough to handle, peel and chop. Heat 1 tbsp of the oil in a non-stick omelette pan 9–10in (23–25cm) in diameter. Put the potatoes, scallion, garlic, and half the parsley in the pan. Cook over medium heat, stirring and tossing, for 5 minutes or until the potatoes are lightly browned at the edges.

Break the eggs into a bowl, season lightly with salt and pepper, and whisk until blended. Spread the potato mixture evenly in the pan. Increase the heat a little and add the remaining 1 tbsp of oil. Pour the egg mixture into the pan. Cook without stirring, but shaking the pan often to prevent sticking, until the omelette is just set.

Remove from the heat. Swirl the butter over the omelette to make it shine, and sprinkle the rest of the chopped parsley over the top. Slip the omelette onto a warmed serving plate, cut into wedges, and serve at once.

Œufs farcis de Pâques

In Provence, as elsewhere in France, eggs—the symbol of new life—have always been at the heart of Easter celebrations. Long before the trend for chocolate eggs, the Provençal Easter Sunday feast traditionally started with a savory dish of stuffed eggs. They still make a popular appetizer.

Bring about 4in (10cm) of water to a boil in a large sauté pan or wide saucepan. Use a slotted spoon to carefully add the eggs. Cook over low heat for 9 minutes. Take them out, refresh under cold running water, and let sit in a bowl of cold water for a couple of minutes. When cool enough to handle, carefully remove the shells—it is easier to start by first cracking the rounded end of the egg.

Put the eggs on a work surface and slice in half lengthwise. Scoop out the yolks with a teaspoon and put in a bowl. Reserve the whites.

Drain and shred the tuna. Using a fork, mash together the yolks and tuna. Stir in the sauce verte. Season with a little pepper.

Using a teaspoon, carefully spoon the mixture into the egg white halves, mounding it generously. Decorate the top of each with half an olive. Arrange on a dish, sprinkle with parsley, and serve. Or, if you like, cover loosely and refrigerate for up to 3 hours before serving.

Serves 6

Preparation 25 minutes
Cooking 10 minutes
6 large eggs
half of a 6oz (175g) can of canned
    tuna in olive oil
2 tbsp Sauce Verte (p129)
    or mayonnaise
freshly ground black pepper
    to taste
6 black olives, pitted and halved
2 scant tbsp finely chopped
    flat-leaf parsley

Œufs farcis aux anchois

Replace the tuna with 3 anchovy fillets in oil, drained and mashed with a fork. Mash the egg yolks with the sauce verte, then stir in the anchovies with 1 heaping tsp of chopped drained capers. Stir in 1 tsp grated lemon zest.

Œufs farcis à la tapenade

Mash the egg yolks with 2 tbsp fresh Brousse cheese or ricotta, a generous grinding of black pepper, and 1 tbsp Tapenade (p117).

Œufs farcis aux tomates

Mash the egg yolks with 1 tbsp Ketchup à la Provençale (p123), 2 tbsp mayonnaise, and 1 tsp finely chopped fresh chives.

Œufs brouillés aux champignons

You can use fresh or dried mushrooms for this dish of scrambled eggs. Fresh porcini (cèpes) are ideal but expensive, so you could use just one or two fresh porcini, or a few dried ones (see below), along with a other assorted mushrooms. Or, try brown (cremini) mushrooms mixed with a selection of wild mushrooms.

Serves 2

Preparation 15 minutes
Cooking 15 minutes
6oz (175g) mushrooms
1 tbsp olive oil
2 tbsp unsalted butter
1 garlic clove, crushed
1 scallion (green onion), chopped
5 medium eggs
fine sea salt and freshly ground
    black pepper to taste

Wipe the mushrooms clean with a damp paper towel, then chop finely. Heat the olive oil in a non-stick medium frying pan. Add 1 tbsp of the butter. Once the butter melts, spread the mushrooms, garlic, and scallions in the pan. Cook over medium heat, stirring occasionally, for 5 minutes or until softened. Remove from the pan and keep warm.

While the mushrooms are cooking, put 4 of the eggs in a bowl. Stir a few times to mix the yolks and whites, then season lightly with salt and pepper. Put the remaining egg in another bowl and stir to blend.

Wipe the frying pan clean with paper towels. Return to low heat and add the remaining tablespoon of butter. Pour in the 4-egg mixture. Stir slowly and constantly until just thickened and scrambled. Taste, adding salt and pepper as needed.

Remove the pan from the heat and pour in the remaining 1-egg mixture and the reserved mushrooms, stirring until the egg is just set. Serve at once.

Variation

To use dried mushrooms, you'll need ¾–1oz (25–30g) when using them alone, or half the amount if mixed with 4oz (115g) of fresh mushrooms. Dried mushrooms need to soak in hot water for 30 minutes before using. Rinse well after soaking and press dry in a clean tea towel or with paper towels.

Brouillade aux tomates

Scrambling eggs along with tomatoes is an easy way to produce a satisfying feast, especially when you add plenty of fresh basil and a bit of butter.

Blanch and skin the tomato (see p90); remove the seeds and chop the flesh. Put the oil in a large non-stick frying pan and set over medium heat. Add the tomato, garlic, and parsley. Cook, stirring frequently, for 5 minutes.

Meanwhile, put the eggs in a bowl and stir a few times to mix the yolks and whites. Season lightly with salt and pepper.

Pour the eggs over the tomato mixture and reduce the heat a little. Stir gently and constantly until the mixture is thickened and scrambled. Adjust the seasonings, sprinkle the basil over the top, and stir in the butter.

While the eggs are cooking, toast the bread and spread with butter. Spoon the scrambled egg mixture over the toast. Serve at once.

Serves 2

Preparation 15 minutes
Cooking 15 minutes

1 medium to large ripe tomato
1 tbsp peanut or sunflower oil
1 garlic clove, crushed
2 tsp finely chopped
  flat-leaf parsley
5 medium eggs
fine sea salt and freshly ground
  black pepper to taste
3 fresh basil leaves, cut into shreds
2 tsp unsalted butter, cut into bits

For the toast
2 thick slices rustic country-style
  bread
unsalted butter, softened for
  spreading

"Take care not to over-stir or over-cook the egg and tomato mixture during cooking—the eggs should still be in soft curds at the end."

dinner

Menu

artichauts
à la barigoule

morue fraîche
sauce raïto

gâteau de pêches
sauce mousseline
au caramel

Preparing artichokes

With their tight leaves and inner choke, artichokes can be intimidating. A member of the thistle family, they can seldom be eaten without extensive trimming, but are well worth the effort. After a little preparation and the help of classic Provençal flavors,

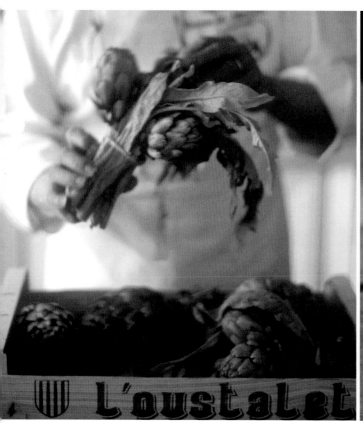 

Choose   The best artichokes have a heavy, firm stem and tight, fresh-looking leaves. Beware of limp stems and dried, yellowing leaves—an indication the artichoke is past its prime. Artichokes do not keep well. Refrigerate them in a plastic bag and cook within 48 hours of purchase.

Trim   Chop off the pointed tip of the artichoke evenly with a sharp, heavy knife, then remove the tough outer leaves. Pull the leaves off firmly, one by one, working with a quick outward movement, then discard. Use a small, sharp knife to trim any coarse pieces around the artichoke base, making it look as neat as possible.

they are a very rewarding ingredient, with a lovely meaty texture. Those prepared with lemon juice can be cooked successfully in the microwave. Cover with plastic wrap and cook on high for 5 minutes; let stand for a minute, then check for tenderness. Return to the microwave if necessary.

Cut   The heart or base of the artichoke, which is called *fond* in French, is the meatiest, most rewarding part. To expose it, cut off all the leaves above it. You will still need to scrape off or scoop out the inedible hairy choke inside. Use a melon baller or a sharp teaspoon to do this.

Rub   Artichokes discolor quickly. To prevent this, gently press the cut side of a lemon half over the artichoke flesh. The citric acid will slow down oxidation—the process that turns exposed cut surfaces brown. A touch of lemon will also enhance the flavor of the cooked artichoke.

Artichauts à la barigoule

This old-fashioned dish of stewed artichokes is best served straight from the pot. The bed of aromatic vegetables and bacon isn't for eating—its job is to give the dish a rich aroma and sweet, wonderful flavor.

Serves 6

Preparation 20 minutes
Cooking 1½ hours

¼lb (115g) button mushrooms
1 thick slice cooked ham
3 shallots, finely chopped
1 cup dry white wine
5 tbsp olive oil
fine sea salt and freshly ground
   black pepper to taste
2 tbsp wine vinegar or lemon juice
6 artichokes
1 lemon, halved
1 large mild onion, chopped
1 carrot, chopped
3 garlic cloves, sliced
1 bay leaf, cut into 4 pieces
1 tsp dried thyme or 1 sprig
   of fresh thyme
2 thick bacon slices, cut into ½in
   (1cm) dice (about ½ cup)
1 small egg

Wipe the mushrooms clean with damp paper towels, then finely chop. Dice the ham. Put the shallots and ½ cup white wine in a sauté pan and cook over low heat until soft and mushy. Add 2 tbsp of the oil and the ham and stir, then add the mushrooms and season with salt and pepper. Stir for a minute. Remove from the heat and set aside.

Fill a bowl with cold water and add the wine vinegar or lemon juice. Prepare the artichokes (see pp146–147), cutting off the stalks level with the base so that the artichokes will stand upright. As each artichoke is prepared, rub it well with the lemon halves and put it upside down into the bowl of water.

Take a heavy sauté pan or Dutch oven that is deep and large enough to hold the artichokes standing snugly side by side. Put in the onion, carrot, garlic, bay leaf, thyme, bacon, remaining ½ cup wine, and 1 cup water. Season with salt and pepper.

Break the egg into the mushroom mixture and stir to mix. Drain the artichokes, shaking them well to remove excess moisture. Spoon the mushroom mixture into the artichoke cups. Place the artichokes upright into the sauté pan. Spoon the remaining 3 tbsp olive oil over the top.

Cover tightly, bring to a simmer, and cook over very low heat for about 1 hour. Leave the artichokes in the covered pan, off the heat, for 5–10 minutes, then serve.

Snap off the large, outer leaves from each artichoke, then trim the base and scoop out the choke.

Morue fraîche, sauce raïto

Rubbing a little salt and sugar into fresh cod gives the fish a slightly firmer texture that is pleasantly reminiscent of traditional salt cod, without its strong briny taste. The red wine sauce called *Raïto* is a classic accompaniment for Provence fish dishes. Serve with mashed or steamed potatoes.

Pat the cod fillets dry with paper towels. Mix together the salt and sugar, and rub all over the fillets. Put them in a dish, cover, and refrigerate for 3 hours.

While the cod is curing, make the sauce. Put the oil in a sauté pan or Dutch oven, add the onions, bay leaves, and fennel, and cook over a low heat for 12–15 minutes until softened, stirring occasionally. Meanwhile, blanch and skin the tomatoes (see p90); remove the seeds, and chop the flesh. Finely chop together the garlic and the leaves from the parsley sprigs.

Add the garlic and parsley to the onions, then stir in the tomatoes. Pour in the red wine, turn up the heat a little, and stir for 3 minutes. Add 2 cups water. Season with salt and pepper and add the sugar. Continue cooking for 5 minutes.

Finely chop together the capers and cornichons. Stir into the mixture and simmer for 10–15 minutes, adding a few more tablespoons of water if the sauce looks too thick. Set aside. Before serving, reheat gently, and discard the fennel and bay leaves.

Rinse the cod fillets several times in cold water. Put in a sauté pan, cover generously with cold water, and season lightly. Bring to a simmer over low heat. Remove from the heat as soon as small bubbles start to appear at the edges of the pan. Drain on paper towels.

Dust the cod with flour and season lightly with salt and pepper. Heat the oil in a frying pan and sauté the cod over medium–high heat for 2–3 minutes on each side until golden, turning the pieces over carefully with a metal spatula.

Serve the fish immediately on warmed plates, with a spoonful or two of the sauce and garnished with olives.

Sprinkle the cod fillets generously with the salt and sugar mixture, then pat in well. This will draw out the moisture.

Serves 4

Preparation 3½ hours
Cooking 30 minutes

4 thick skinless cod fillets, about 2lb (900g) total weight
2 tbsp coarse sea salt
2 tbsp sugar
fine sea salt and freshly ground black pepper to taste
flour for dusting
2½ tbsp olive oil
pitted black olives for garnish

For the raïto sauce
2 tbsp olive oil
2 medium onions, finely chopped
2 bay leaves
3 stalks of dried fennel or 1 tbsp fennel seed tied in cheesecloth
3 medium ripe tomatoes
3 garlic cloves
3 sprigs of flat-leaf parsley
⅔ cup red wine
1 tsp sugar
2 tsp drained small capers
2 small cornichons (tart gherkins)

Gâteau de pêches, sauce mousseline au caramel

With their smooth skin and delicate flavor, nectarines are a lovely member of the peach family. Unlike velvety peaches with their slightly thicker skins, nectarines don't need to be peeled. For this cake with a smooth caramel sauce, use whichever fruit looks better at the market.

Serves 6

Preparation 30 minutes
Cooking 50 minutes

4 large, ripe but firm nectarines
  or peaches
1½ tbsp unsalted butter, plus
  extra for greasing
3 large eggs
½ cup sugar
1 cup heavy (whipping) cream
1 heaping tbsp cornstarch
1½ tsp baking powder
1½ cups ground almonds
flour for dusting
Sauce Mousseline au Caramel
  (p134) to serve

Dip the nectarines into a pot of boiling water and blanch for 1–2 minutes. Drain and refresh under cold water (peel if using peaches). Cut each fruit into 10–12 segments and discard the pits. Drain in a colander while you prepare the cake mixture.

Preheat the oven to 375F°/190°C. Butter a 9in (23cm) moule à manqué tin or a non-stick round cake tin. Line the bottom with parchment paper, then butter again and dust with flour.

Combine the eggs and sugar in a bowl. With an electric mixer, beat for 5 minutes until pale and thick. Mix in the cream, then sift in the cornstarch and baking powder. Mix in the ground almonds. Set aside.

Melt the butter in a frying pan and cook the nectarines over medium heat for 3 minutes or until just tinged with gold. Drain on paper towels.

Scrape half the cake mixture into the prepared tin. Add the drained nectarines in a neat layer, then pour the rest of the cake mixture over the top. Bake for 25 minutes. Reduce the heat to 325°F/160°C and continue baking for 15–20 minutes. A metal skewer inserted into the center of the cake should come out clean. Let cool 10–15 minutes before unmolding and peeling off the parchment paper.

Serve barely warm or at room temperature, with chilled sauce mousseline.

Thickly slice the nectarines, leaving the smooth skins on, and then sauté in butter to color them a delicate gold.

thursday

Fresh meat was a

rare luxury throughout much of the long history of Provence. Cattle was kept for milk and cheese, and chicken for eggs, with wild birds and game occasionally supplementing the contents of the cooking pot. Find out how local cooks excel at slowly nurturing tougher cuts into tender aromatic stews.

Viandes et volailles

In the frugal diet of old Provence, when most people existed on vegetables and fruit, meat was a treat only to be enjoyed on special occasions. Provençal cooks still treat their meat and poultry with common sense, respect... and plenty of herbs.

Shooting is popular and small wild birds like thrushes, partridges, and quail often find their way onto the grill or into the pot.

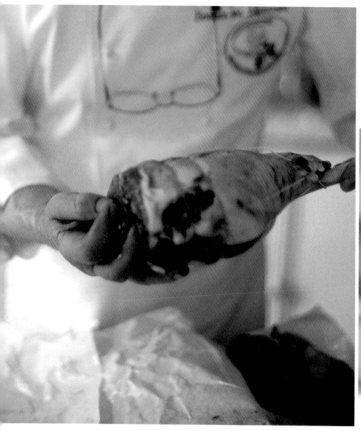

An enduring favorite for a festive table is a leg of Sisteron lamb. The lambs are a small, stocky local breed whose happy lot in life is to graze aromatic wild herbs in the foothills of the Southern Alps. They are butchered at four months—later than most—which gives the meat time to develop a deep, fragrant flavor and a sweet, fleshy texture.

"A bouquet of fresh herbs, plenty of garlic, and a ribbon of orange peel always work wonders. Don't be shy about using alternatives—meat dishes like daubes can be just as tasty with lamb as with beef."

Roast beef is a rare treat, and it is the less expensive, slower-cooking cuts that best suit the highly aromatic local cooking style.

Provençal cooks are thrifty: their fondness for stuffing ingredients to make dishes stretch further extends to meat and poultry too. Adding a substantial stuffing to a duck means that you have to roast it or pot roast it slowly, which ensures the flesh stays beautifully tender. The secret is to use plenty of intensely flavored herbs.

Infusion de romarin

Herb and wine-based infusions make an ideal cooking medium for meats. Start by simmering herbs in water to produce a strong tea-like concoction, then pour in a generous amount of wine. Bring to a boil and let it bubble away, to allow the alcohol to evaporate and the raw taste of the wine to disappear. The flavors will mellow and develop and the infusion can then be used just like a stock. The infusion here is redolent of rosemary and makes an ideal cooking liquid for lamb in the recipe for Agneau Confit au Miel (p161).

Makes about 5½ cups

Preparation 15 minutes
Cooking 1 hour
2 bunches fresh rosemary sprigs
4 bay leaves
6 juniper berries
2in (5cm) piece dried orange peel
  (see pp328–329)
1 bottle (750ml) rosé wine

Put the rosemary, bay leaves, juniper berries, and orange peel in a saucepan with 5½ cups boiling water. Reduce the heat to very low and cook for 15 minutes to infuse the flavors.

Add the wine to the infusion, increase the heat to medium–high, and cook until the liquid has reduced by one-third.

Strain the reduced rosemary and wine infusion through a sieve into a bowl.

To use, simply pour some or all of the infusion into the pan after browning the meat. Alternatively, for lighter poached dishes and leaner cuts of meat, rinse the meat in cold water with a little vinegar or lemon juice and pat dry. Bring the infusion to a simmer and add the raw meat. Whether the meat is raw or browned, once you've added it to the infusion, keep the heat moderate and do not let the liquid boil.

Variations
When cold, infusions can be used as a marinade. Simply add the meat, cover, and marinate in the fridge for at least 6 hours or overnight. The mixture of wine and herbs will tenderize and flavor the meat. Strain the marinade after you've lifted out the meat and reheat before using as described above. You can also add a few tablespoons of this infusion to sauces for extra flavoring.

"Some infusion marriages are made in heaven: rosemary and rosé wine for lamb... thyme and sweet white wine for rabbit... thyme or summer savory and dry white wine for pork... sage and dry white wine for veal... parsley, bay leaves, and red wine for beef... tarragon and white wine for chicken..."

Agneau confit au miel et au vin rosé

This sweetest of lamb stews, with honey and rosé wine, is nicely supported by the clean woodsy flavor of rosemary. Serve it with creamy carrots with green olives (p76). Both dishes take some time to prepare but they can be cooked ahead and gently reheated before serving.

Cut the lamb into nine or ten pieces. Brush the lamb with the honey and season lightly with salt and pepper. Place a large sauté pan or flameproof casserole over medium heat. Add the olive oil, then the lamb and cook, turning once or twice, for 8–10 minutes or until the meat is nicely browned all over.

Add the shallots, garlic, carrots, celery, and onions. Stir well and season with salt, pepper, and nutmeg. Continue cooking, partially covered, over very low heat for 10–15 minutes.

Gradually ladle the rosemary infusion into the pan and stir to keep the lamb just covered with liquid as it barely simmers. Keep the pan partially covered between additions and keep the heat very low. Allow up to 2 hours for the lamb to cook very gently in the infusion, stirring from time to time. Adjust the seasonings.

Garnish with sprigs of fresh rosemary just before serving.

Serves 4

Preparation 15 minutes
Cooking 2½ hours
1 shoulder of lamb, about 3lb
  (1.3kg), boned
¼ cup rosemary honey
fine sea salt and freshly ground
  black pepper to taste
¼ cup olive oil
½lb (225g) shallots, finely
  chopped
5 garlic cloves, thinly sliced
1lb (450g) carrots, peeled
  and sliced
1 celery rib, diced
20 boiling onions, peeled
1 tsp grated fresh nutmeg
5½ cups Infusion de Romarin
  (p158)
a few sprigs of fresh rosemary
  to garnish

Brush rosemary honey over the lamb before searing to give the meat a richly caramelized crust.

Gigot d'agneau aux aromates

For this slow-cooked aromatic leg of lamb, allow at least 1lb (450g) of meat per person, because lamb shrinks considerably during cooking. This may sound extravagant but you don't need to buy top quality lamb for this dish—slow cooking works its magic even on tougher cuts.

Serves 6-8

Preparation 15 minutes
Cooking 5 hours, in stages
1 bottle (750ml) white dessert
    wine, such as a muscat or late
    harvest Riesling
6 bay leaves
several sprigs of fresh rosemary
a few sprigs of fresh thyme
1 large head of garlic, split into
    unpeeled cloves
1 large leg of lamb, 5½–6½lb
    (2.5–3kg)
fine sea salt and freshly ground
    black pepper to taste
1 tbsp ground cumin
¼ cup olive oil
finely grated zest and juice
    of 1 lemon
½ cup light cream or half-and-half

Bring the wine to a simmer in a saucepan with the bay leaves, a few sprigs of rosemary and thyme, and 3 of the garlic cloves.

Meanwhile, season the lamb and rub with 1½ tsp of cumin. Heat 2 tbsp of the olive oil in a flameproof casserole just large enough to contain the lamb. Add the lamb and cook, turning occasionally, over medium–high heat until nicely browned all over.

Pour in the hot wine and flavorings and return to a simmer. As soon as the liquid simmers, reduce the heat to very low, cover, and cook gently for 2 hours. Lift the lid from time to time to make sure the wine is barely simmering, and skim off any foam that rises to the surface.

Preheat the oven to 300°F/150°C. Lift the lamb out of the pot and put it in a large bowl. Strain the cooking liquid through a sieve into another bowl and reserve.

Return the lamb to the cooking pot and season with the remaining 1½ tsp cumin and the lemon zest. Add the remaining garlic cloves and a little more rosemary and drizzle with the remaining 2 tbsp olive oil and the lemon juice. Cook in the oven for 1½ hours.

Take the casserole out of the oven. Turn the leg of lamb over and stir to distribute the garlic and herbs. Moisten with a ladleful of the reserved cooking liquid. Return to the oven, uncovered, to cook for 45 minutes or until the lamb is meltingly tender.

Remove from the oven. Lift out the garlic cloves and cover the lamb loosely to keep warm. Pour the rest of the reserved cooking liquid into a saucepan, add the garlic, and bring to a simmer, stirring and mashing the garlic to extract as much flavor as possible.

Transfer the lamb to a warmed serving platter and garnish with a little fresh rosemary. Cover again to keep warm. Pour the cooking liquid and garlic into the casserole, and cook over medium heat, stirring and scraping up any browned bits. Pour the liquid back into the saucepan. Stir in the cream and cook for 1 minute. Adjust the seasonings. Strain the sauce through a sieve into a warmed sauceboat.

Spoon a little sauce over the lamb and serve as soon as possible.

Côtes d'agneau grillées

Cooking in the hearth—or on a barbecue or even spit roasting over a fire—may be a technique as old as the hills, but it is still a little tricky. You need to watch the meat as it cooks, and trust your nose, eyes, and instincts. For lamb chops to be cooked over an open fire, you should select large chops with a fair amount of fat. When eating them, hold them in your fingers, which adds to the enjoyment.

Serves 4

Preparation 5 minutes
Cooking 4-8 minutes
8–12 large, thick loin (T-bone), rib,
  or sirloin lamb chops
fine sea salt and freshly ground
  black pepper

Trim the chops to neaten their appearance. Season lightly with salt and pepper.

Place the chops over the fire, preferably in a wire basket, keeping them about 4in (10cm) from the flames. After 3–5 minutes, turn the chops over, move them a little further away from the flames, and sprinkle with salt. Cook for 1–2 minutes longer, depending on how pink you like your lamb.

Check for doneness, and season with pepper and a little more salt if needed. Let rest for a couple of minutes before eating.

Trim the lamb chops and arrange them side by side in a wire grilling basket, then cook in the hearth until browned and crisp but still pink and juicy within.

Crespeou

Cut this savory layered omelette cake into wedges and serve with a salad or vegetable dish such as zucchini with lemon and cilantro (see opposite) for lunch. The omelette also makes a good appetizer, cut into cubes and skewered with toothpicks. Or you could serve it as a starter with black olives on the side.

Serves 4

Preparation 10 minutes
Cooking 20 minutes

½ red bell pepper
1 tbsp soft unsalted butter, plus a little extra to finish
9 large eggs
fine sea salt and freshly ground black pepper to taste
leaves from 4–5 sprigs of fresh basil, chopped
a small handful of fresh chives, chopped
3 strips of thick-cut bacon, cut into dice, or crosswise into ½in (1cm) strips
2½ tbsp peanut oil

Preheat the oven to 375°F/190°C. Line a baking sheet with foil.

Remove seeds from the red pepper, then chop finely. Melt the butter in a small non-stick frying pan, about 5–6in (12.5–15cm) in diameter, and cook the red pepper 5–7 minutes until softened. Remove from the heat.

Break 3 eggs into each of three bowls. Season each lightly and whisk until frothy. Add the red pepper to one bowl and stir to mix. Stir the basil and chives into the second bowl.

Wipe the frying pan clean with a paper towel. Put the bacon in the pan and cook over medium heat for 3–5 minutes until crisp and golden. Spread on paper towels to drain, then stir into the third bowl of beaten eggs.

Wipe the pan clean again. Return to a fairly high heat and add half the oil.

Lightly whisk the red pepper and egg mixture. Turn into the pan and cook, lifting the edges and tilting the pan over the heat to enable the egg mixture to spread out as it cooks. Once the omelette is just set but still very moist, lift it onto the foil-lined baking sheet.

Lightly whisk the bacon and egg mixture. Add a little more oil to the frying pan and cook a second omelette in the same way as the first. Stack this omelette on top of the red pepper omelette.

Now cook the basil and chive omelette. Place it on top of the others and swirl a little butter over the surface to make it shine. Put the layered omelette in the oven to heat through for 5 minutes.

Remove from the oven and let cool for a few minutes. Serve the layered omelette warm or at room temperature, cut into wedges.

Courgettes fraîches à la coriandre

Fresh zucchini ribbons dressed with lemon and cilantro make a lovely summer offering, served as a starter or a side dish with an omelette or grilled or barbecued fish, lamb, or chicken. Be sure to drain the zucchini well before you add the olive oil and cilantro—it does wonders for their texture and taste.

Cut off and discard the ends of the zucchini. Using a vegetable peeler, cut the zucchini lengthwise into long, thin ribbons. Alternatively, if you prefer, shred the zucchini, using the large holes on a box grater or grating disc of a food processor. Put the zucchini in a colander, season with salt, sprinkle with the lemon juice, and toss gently to mix.

Cover the colander and set inside a bowl. Let sit in a cool place to marinate for at least 2 hours, or overnight in the refrigerator, if time allows.

Remove the bowl and stand the colander in the sink. Press down the zucchini with the palms of your hands. Let drain for 10–15 minutes, pressing down a few times.

Put the zucchini in a serving dish, drizzle with olive oil, and scatter the cilantro leaves over the top. Toss and season with pepper. Serve soon.

Serves 4-6

Preparation 15 minutes,
  plus marinating
8 medium zucchini
fine sea salt and freshly ground
  black pepper to taste
juice of ½ lemon
4–6 tbsp extra virgin olive oil
leaves from 4 sprigs of fresh
  cilantro

"Use freshly picked zucchini for this recipe—there is no cooking method that can improve the taste of old, dry vegetables. Look for zucchini no longer than 5in (12cm). Larger ones tend to be less firm."

Côtes de porc grillées à la sauge

Marinating pork chops in a mixture of grainy Dijon mustard and sage gets them off to a very good start before grilling. They will come out tender and well flavored—grill them over indirect heat outdoors, on a cooktop grill pan, or under a moderately hot broiler to make sure they have time to cook thoroughly.

Serves 4

Preparation 5 minutes,
 plus marinating
Cooking 20 minutes
4 large, thick pork chops
fine sea salt and freshly ground
 black pepper to taste
3½ tbsp grainy Dijon mustard
¼ cup olive oil
10 fresh sage leaves

Cut slits in the fat at regular intervals around the pork chops, and season lightly all over with salt and pepper.

In a small bowl, mix together the mustard and oil. Coarsely chop and stir in 6 of the sage leaves. Arrange the chops in a shallow dish and brush both sides with the mustard mixture. Cover and refrigerate for at least 6 hours or overnight.

Before cooking, return the chops to room temperature.

In Provence, the chops would be cooked in the hearth over pine cones for about 20 minutes, turned over regularly, and kept about 4in (10cm) from the fire. Alternatively, grill over indirect heat or broil 6in from the flame, turning once, until cooked through but still juicy inside, about 15 minutes total.

Season with a little extra pepper and garnish each chop with a fresh sage leaf.

Slash the fat on the edges of the chops so they don't curl during cooking, then coat them all over with mustard and sage, and set aside to marinate.

Estouffade de porc

The Provencal word *estoufa*, literally "to smother," aptly describes the technique used in this recipe for pork pot roast with herbs, onions, and orange. The meat is slowly simmered in a tightly covered casserole, a process that works wonders on even the toughest cuts, and the end result is tender and fragrant. Like many slow-cooked dishes, this tastes even better reheated.

Serves 6

Preparation 15 minutes
Cooking about 3 hours

3–4 tbsp olive oil
1 boned and rolled loin of
   pork, 3–4lb (1.3–1.8kg), excess
   fat removed
2 large mild onions, thinly sliced
3 garlic cloves, crushed
fine sea salt and freshly ground
   black pepper to taste
1 tsp paprika
1 tbsp Dijon mustard
2 bay leaves, crumbled
6 fresh sage leaves
2 small sprigs of fresh thyme
1 large, ripe tomato, chopped
1 bottle (750ml) dry white wine
grated zest and juice of 1 orange

Heat the oil in a large, heavy flameproof casserole or Dutch oven until extremely hot but not smoking. Brown the pork on all sides, then remove from the pot.

Reduce the heat to low and add the onions and garlic. Cook for 10 minutes, stirring occasionally, until they are soft but not browned. Meanwhile, season the pork with salt, pepper, and paprika, rubbing them in well.

Return the pork to the pot. Stir in the mustard, herbs, and tomato. Cover and cook over low heat for 5–10 minutes. Turn the pork over and cook, covered, for another 5 minutes.

Pour in the wine. Put the lid back on and cook over very low heat for at least 2 hours until the pork is tender—the exact timing will depend upon the age and quality of the meat you use. Keep the pot very tightly covered and cook over low heat, turning the pork occasionally. Add the orange zest and juice after 1 hour.

Adjust the seasoning with a little pepper at the end of cooking.

"In true Provence spirit, you can replace the pork with kid, but not goat meat, which tends to be too tough."

Soupe courte

The fact that there usually isn't much liquid left at the end of cooking may well have inspired the name for this traditional Provence meat and pasta stew—*soupe courte* means "short soup." Rich gelatinous breast of veal gives the dish a sweet, deep flavor.

Cut the veal into 12 pieces. Season the meat. Put the olive oil in a flameproof casserole or Dutch oven, add the pieces of veal, and cook over medium heat for 10 minutes or until browned all over.

Meanwhile, blanch and skin the tomatoes (see p90), then chop the flesh.

Add the onion to the veal and cook for a few minutes, stirring frequently, until lightly browned and softened. Add the garlic, parsley sprigs, bay leaves, and tomatoes. Season with salt and pepper and add 4 cups water.

Bring to a simmer, then cover the pot and reduce the heat to low. Cook for 50 minutes or until the meat is just tender.

Uncover the pot, increase the heat a little, and add the macaroni. Cook uncovered, stirring a few times, for 10–12 minutes (or according to package instructions) until the macaroni is tender.

Adjust the seasonings and sprinkle with chopped parsley. Serve from the casserole, and pass a bowl of grated Gruyère cheese at the table.

Variation

Instead of veal breast, use boned and trimmed lamb shoulder, cut into 12 pieces. The lamb will take a little less time to cook than the veal—about 40 minutes before you add the macaroni.

Serves 6–8

Preparation 20 minutes
Cooking 1¾ hours
1 boneless breast of veal, about
    2¼lb (1kg)
fine sea salt and freshly ground
    black pepper to taste
6 tbsp olive oil
4 ripe medium tomatoes
1 large mild onion, thinly sliced
3 garlic cloves, crushed
3 sprigs of flat-leaf parsley
3 bay leaves
8–9oz (250g) elbow macaroni

To serve
2 tbsp finely chopped
    flat-leaf parsley
4oz (125g) shredded Gruyère
    cheese

Côtes de veau aux pignons

Pine nuts give this old-fashioned dish a distinctive Provençal accent. Plumped up with port and cream during cooking, they are delicious with the tender veal chops and contrast nicely with the mushrooms.

Wipe the mushrooms clean with damp paper towels, then slice them thinly.

Place a large frying pan over medium–high heat, and melt the butter. Season the chops with salt and pepper, then cook in the hot butter for 10 minutes, turning once, until golden brown. Lift the chops onto a plate.

Drain off any excess cooking fat, then put the chops back in the pan. Add the port and cook over medium heat, scraping up any browned bits from the pan, until bubbling.

Pour in ½ cup water. Increase the heat a little and stir until simmering again. Stir in the mushrooms, then the pine nuts and cream.

Reduce the heat to medium and cook, stirring occasionally, for 5 minutes or until the sauce thickens. Reduce the heat to low, partially cover the pan, and cook 10 minutes longer. Adjust the seasonings.

Place the chops and mushrooms on a warmed serving platter and drizzle the sauce over all. Scatter parsley leaves over the top and serve at once.

Serves 4

Preparation 10 minutes
Cooking 30 minutes
½lb (225g) button mushrooms
2 tbsp soft unsalted butter
4 large veal chops
fine sea salt and freshly ground
  black pepper to taste
⅓ cup tawny port
⅓ cup pine nuts
½ cup light cream or half and half
flat-leaf parsley leaves to garnish

Sauté the veal chops in butter to brown both sides well before adding the port and mushrooms.

Poulet rôti à l'ail

Not surprisingly, the preferred Provençal way of roasting chicken is with plenty of garlic. Whether you use garlic or not, the roasting method in this recipe produces tender chicken with a crisp skin. If cooking without garlic, simply add an extra tablespoon of herbs and a little more cream and wine to the sauce.

Serves 4-6

Preparation 15 minutes
Cooking about 2 hours

1 free-range chicken, about
    3¼lb (1.5kg), at cool room
    temperature
1 heaping tbsp mixed fresh herbs
    (thyme and marjoram or oregano
    and rosemary)
1 garlic clove, crushed
1 tsp finely grated lemon zest
2 tbsp soft unsalted butter
fine sea salt and freshly ground
    black pepper to taste
3 tbsp olive oil, plus extra
    to drizzle
3 heads of garlic
⅓ cup dry white wine
3 tbsp light cream or half-and-half

Preheat the oven to 450°F/230°C. Rinse the chicken under cold running water and pat dry with paper towels. In a cup, combine the herbs, crushed garlic, and lemon zest with the butter. Season with a little salt and plenty of pepper.

Spoon half of the butter mixture into the cavity of the chicken. Stir the olive oil into the remaining half. Using a pastry brush, smear the oily mixture all over the outside of the chicken. Season again with salt and pepper. Place the chicken on its side on a rack in a roasting pan.

Put each head of garlic in the center of a piece of aluminum foil. Drizzle 1–2 tsp of olive oil over each head and season lightly with salt and pepper, then bring up the edges of the foil to make neat parcels. Add the garlic parcels to the roasting pan.

Roast for 10 minutes, then turn the chicken onto its other side and roast for another 10 minutes. Turn the chicken breast side down and roast 10 minutes longer.

Reduce the heat to 350°F/180°C. Turn the chicken breast side up and continue roasting for about 1¼ hours. Baste a few times with the cooking juices.

Remove the garlic parcels. Let sit until cool enough to handle, then open them. Separate the garlic cloves and squeeze each one between your thumb and index finger to extract the soft garlic flesh. Put this in a cup and reserve.

Before you turn off the oven, push a skewer into the thickest part of a chicken leg to check that the cooking juices are running clear. Drain the cavity juices (they too should be golden and clear) into the roasting pan and set the chicken on a carving board or plate. Cover loosely with foil and let rest in a warm place while you make the sauce.

Drain off some of the fat from the roasting pan. Place the pan over high heat and pour in the wine and ⅓ cup of water. Boil until reduced by one-third, stirring and scraping the bottom of the pan to dislodge any browned bits. Once the pan is deglazed, add the garlic and cook, stirring, until bubbling hot. Check the seasoning and stir in the cream. Strain through a sieve, or simply pour into a heated sauceboat. Serve the chicken with the sauce as soon as possible.

Bagnet

Bagnet is named after the Provençal verb *bagna*, which means to dip, soak, or immerse. A genuine dipping sauce with a lively flavor, it is used to accompany poached meats, such as the chicken dish on p181. Bagnet can be stored for up to 48 hours in the refrigerator. Allow about 3 tablespoons per serving.

Blanch and skin the tomatoes (see p90); cut in half and remove the seeds, then finely chop the flesh. Place in a bowl.

Combine the garlic, parsley, and basil and chop finely. Add to the tomatoes.

Add the mustard and vinegar. Season with salt. Toss together gently with a fork.

Gradually add the olive oil, whisking with the fork until well blended. Taste and adjust the seasonings with salt and pepper. Keep the sauce, tightly covered, in the refrigerator until needed.

Serve cold. Whisk again just before serving.

Makes 1¼ cups

Preparation 15 minutes
6 medium to large vine-ripened
   tomatoes
5 garlic cloves, smashed
leaves from 7 sprigs of
   flat-leaf parsley
12 fresh basil leaves
1 tsp Dijon mustard
3 tbsp red wine vinegar
fine sea salt and freshly ground
   black pepper to taste
¾ cup olive oil

"This little sauce is packed with flavor. To enjoy your chicken in the pot *à la provençale*, place a couple of generous dollops of bagnet over the chicken and vegetables. The sauce is also very good with poached beef or veal."

Poule au pot et son bagnet

This poached chicken with its tomato dipping sauce is as unpretentious as it is delicious. It's a country dish, traditionally prepared with a large mature bird. Because it is so simple, to cook it successfully you need to use a chicken that has lived a full and happy free-ranging life. Bland standard chickens will produce disappointing results. The cooking liquid will make a fantastic light stock. Strain it and use in sauces and soups, and for cooking meats and rice.

Put the chicken in a very large pot and pour in enough cold water to cover by at least 2in (5cm). Place over medium heat, partially covered.

Meanwhile, char the unpeeled onions and garlic over a gas flame, or under a hot broiler, until blistered and well charred all over. Add to the pot with the chicken.

As soon as foam rises to the surface, start skimming and discarding it. After about 50 minutes, the water should begin to simmer. Add the bouquet garni, cloves, and parsley sprigs. Season with salt and pepper. Continue skimming regularly as the liquid simmers gently over medium heat.

After the chicken has been simmering for about 1 hour, add the carrots, leeks, turnips, and small onions. Continue cooking and skimming for about 20 minutes.

Meanwhile, cut the cabbage into 6 wedges. Using a ladle, remove some of the cooking liquid from the chicken to a smaller saucepan and bring to a boil. Add the cabbage wedges and cook for 15–20 minutes or until tender.

Lift out the cooked chicken. Put into a warmed shallow bowl or rimmed platter and ladle over a little of the cooking liquid. Lift out the peeled vegetables and add to the bowl. Lift out the cabbage wedges, arrange with the other vegetables, and season with a little pepper. Moisten with a little more of the cooking liquid.

Pour some cooking liquid into a warmed sauceboat. Serve the chicken and vegetables with the cooking liquid and the bagnet.

Serves 6

Preparation 20 minutes
Cooking 3 hours
1 large free-range chicken,
   3–3½lb (1.3–1.6kg)
large mild onions, unpeeled
1 head of garlic, unpeeled and
   left whole
bouquet garni made with 2 celery
   ribs, 3 bay leaves, and 1 sprig of
   fresh thyme (see pp28–29)
6 cloves
4 sprigs of flat-leaf parsley
fine sea salt and freshly ground
   black pepper to taste
6 carrots, peeled
6 small to medium leeks
6 baby turnips, peeled
6 small onions, peeled
1 curly green cabbage, such as
   savoy
Bagnet (p179) to serve

Grill the whole onions and head of garlic until blackened but not burned They will give a rich color to the stock and a light smoky flavor.

Pintade aux olives

Guinea fowl is a lean bird with a mildly gamey flavor. In this dish it is sautéed with white wine and herbs, and finished with green olives. The recipe also works well with duck or free-range chicken pieces, or halved pigeons.

Serves 3-4

Preparation 15 minutes
Cooking 1½ hours
1 large ready-to-cook guinea hen
   or fowl, cut up
fine sea salt and freshly ground
   black pepper to taste
1 tbsp olive oil
2 tbsp unsalted butter
1¼ cups dry white wine
3 sprigs of fresh thyme
1 bay leaf
2 medium to large tomatoes
1 large mild onion, finely chopped
1 cup green olives, pitted

Season the pieces of guinea hen. In a large, heavy-based saucepan or Dutch oven, heat the oil and butter. Cook the pieces over medium heat, turning once or twice, until the skin is crisp and golden.

Spoon a couple of tablespoons of the hot fat into a frying pan and discard the rest.

Add the wine and herbs to the guinea hen, cover the pan, and reduce the heat to low. Cook for about 30 minutes, basting once or twice with the pan juices.

Meanwhile, blanch and skin the tomatoes (see p90); remove the seeds and chop the flesh fairly finely. Heat the fat in the frying pan and sauté the tomatoes and onion over low heat, stirring occasionally, until softened. Season lightly.

Stir the onion and tomato into the pan with the guinea hen, then cover again and simmer over low heat for another 30 minutes.

Meanwhile, blanch the olives in a small saucepan of boiling water for 3 minutes. Drain, refresh under cold running water, and drain again.

Add the olives to the guinea hen. Pour in a little water if the mixture looks too dry. Cover and simmer for 5 minutes. Serve very hot.

"Blanching green olives before you add them to the dish gets rid of any briny or bitter flavor, making them taste milder and cleaner."

Lapin chasseur

Hunter's rabbit was probably created when a sportsman put a rabbit he had trapped into a pot, or on a spit over a fire, and accompanied it with wild mushrooms and herbs he had gathered nearby. The same recipe can be used to cook chicken.

Put half of the butter in a sauté pan. Dice and chill the rest of the butter. Add the oil to the pan and heat. Cook the rabbit pieces with the shallots and garlic over medium heat, turning the pieces so they brown evenly.

Sprinkle the rabbit pieces with the flour. Add the brandy and ignite carefully. When the flame subsides, add the white wine and enough chicken stock just to cover the rabbit—adding water, if necessary. Stir well. Season. Cover and simmer over medium heat for 20–30 minutes. Shake the pan occasionally during the cooking to prevent sticking.

Meanwhile, blanch and skin the tomatoes (see p90); remove the seeds and chop the flesh. Wipe the mushrooms clean with damp paper towel, then slice them thinly.

Stir the tomatoes and mushrooms into the pan. Cover and simmer for 10 minutes or until the rabbit pieces are tender and cooked through.

Remove the rabbit from the pan and arrange the pieces on a warm serving platter. Keep warm while you finish the sauce.

Increase the heat under the pan to medium–high. Snip the chives and tarragon into the sauce and cook, stirring, for 1–2 minutes, then swirl in the chilled diced butter. Check the seasoning. Pour the sauce over the rabbit and serve immediately.

Serves 4

Preparation 15 minutes
Cooking 1 hour

3 tbsp unsalted butter
2 tbsp olive oil
1 medium rabbit, cut up
4 small shallots, finely chopped
2 garlic cloves, crushed
1 tbsp flour
3 tbsp brandy
½ cup dry white wine
about 1 cup chicken stock
fine sea salt and freshly ground
    black pepper to taste
2 ripe medium tomatoes
¼ lb (115g) brown (cremini)
    mushrooms
several sprigs each of fresh chives
    and tarragon

Cailles rôties au Noilly

Quail is a popular bird in Provence. Roasting them with Noilly Prat and thyme recreates the aromas of their natural habitat and of the wild scented shrubs of the Provence hills. Dry vermouth makes an excellent cooking medium: as a fortified wine it has an enduring pervasive flavor that is good with poultry, white meats, and fish (use as a substitute for pastis if you don't enjoy the flavor of anise).

Serves 4

Preparation 10 minutes
Cooking 1 hour

6 tbsp (¾ stick) soft unsalted
  butter
4 tsp tiny leaves plucked from
  sprigs of fresh thyme
fine sea salt and freshly ground
  black pepper to taste
8 ready-to-cook quail
2 tbsp olive oil
8 thin slices of streaky smoked
  bacon, chopped
3 medium shallots, finely chopped
6 juniper berries
½ cup Noilly Prat or other dry
  white vermouth

Preheat the oven to 350°F/180°C. Using a fork, mash together the butter and thyme. Season. Spread the butter mixture over the quail. Put them in a small roasting pan with a tight-fitting lid. Alternatively, cut a piece of heavy-duty aluminum foil large enough to cover the pan.

Heat a non-stick medium frying pan. Add the olive oil, then the bacon, shallots, and juniper berries. Cook over medium heat for 5 minutes.

Pour the vermouth over the quail. Scatter the bacon and shallot mixture over the top. Cover and roast for 40 minutes or until just tender.

Remove the lid and roast uncovered for 5 minutes. Remove from the oven and let rest for 5 minutes before serving.

Steak au beurre d'anchois

Anchovy butter gives this quick steak recipe a nice Provençal edge. All the quantities can easily be doubled to serve four people. Use either a very large frying pan or two medium pans to cook the four steaks at the same time.

Lightly season the steaks with salt and pepper and set aside.

To make the anchovy butter, put the shallot, parsley, garlic, anchovies, and brandy in a food processor (preferably with a small bowl). Pulse quickly to a coarse purée, then scrape down the sides of the bowl with a spatula. Add the butter and process to blend. Taste and adjust the seasonings with pepper. Set aside.

Heat the olive oil in a frying pan. Cook the steaks in the hot pan for 1½–3 minutes on each side, depending upon how well done you like your meat. Lift the steaks out of the pan onto warmed plates.

Carefully wipe the pan clean with a thick wedge of paper towels (take care as the pan will be very hot). Return the pan to the heat. Add the anchovy butter and cook just until melted, then spoon or pour over the steaks. Season with pepper and serve.

Serves 2

Preparation 15 minutes
Cooking 5 minutes
2 beef filet mignon steaks, about
   6oz (175g) each
fine sea salt and freshly ground
   black pepper to taste
1 tbsp olive oil
For the anchovy butter
½ shallot, finely chopped
1 tbsp chopped flat-leaf parsley
1 garlic clove, crushed
2 anchovy fillets in oil, drained
1 tsp brandy
4 tbsp (½ stick) soft unsalted
   butter

"Like other flavored butters, anchovy butter can be prepared ahead (see recipe p132) and stored in the refrigerator or freezer, ready to produce quick dishes, Provençal style."

dinner

Menu

daube de bœuf
à la
provençale

macaronade
—

figues rôties
à la crème

La marinade

There's nothing complicated about marinades—they just take a little time to work their magic. The list of ingredients may be long but each of the elements plays its own part. This marinade is traditional for a beef daube (see p192). It can also be used for lamb.

Makes enough for 4-5lb (1.8-2.3kg) meat

Preparation 30 minutes

5 garlic cloves, sliced

3 carrots, sliced

2 celery ribs, chopped

2 large onions, chopped

3in (7cm) strip of dried orange peel (see pp328–329)

3 sprigs of fresh parsley

2 sprigs of fresh thyme

2 bay leaves

1 tsp tiny fresh savory leaves

½ tsp grated fresh nutmeg

12 black peppercorns, crushed

4 juniper berries, crushed

4 whole cloves

2 tbsp red wine vinegar

1 bottle (750ml) robust dry red wine

fine sea salt and freshly ground black pepper to taste

Put the meat in a shallow dish or bowl. Add the garlic, carrots, celery, and onions. Add the orange peel, herbs, and spices.

Pour in the vinegar and wine. Season with salt and pepper and gently stir so the pieces of meat are mixed with the liquid and flavorings. Cover and let marinate in a cool room up to 2 hours, or refrigerate overnight.

Lift out the meat. Strain the marinade through a large sieve placed over a bowl. According to the recipe instructions, reserve both the solid ingredients and the liquid separately.

"Whether simple and basic, or complex, marinating meat before cooking is a good way to make it more tender, speed up the actual cooking, and develop flavors. The longer the marinating time, the more powerful its effect."

Daube de bœuf à la provençale

You don't need to be the proud owner of a *daubière* (see p37) to make a daube (Provençal slow-cooked beef), but without a strip of dried orange peel in the red wine marinade, a daube just wouldn't be authentic.

Serves 6

Preparation and cooking
   4½ hours, plus marinating
   overnight

4½lb (2kg) boneless stewing beef,
   such as chuck or bottom round
La Marinade (p190), chilled or at
   room temperature
2 tbsp olive oil
½lb (225g) thick-cut bacon, cut
   crosswise into ½in (1cm) strips
   (lardons)
1 large mild onion, chopped
2 tbsp flour
fine sea salt and freshly ground
   black pepper to taste

Cut the beef into 2in (5cm) chunks. Put them in a large bowl and cover with the marinade. Cover and marinate in the refrigerator overnight.

Remove the beef from the bowl and blot dry with paper towels. Set aside.

Strain the marinade through a sieve set over a bowl. Reserve both the liquid in the bowl and the solid ingredients in the sieve separately.

Place a large sauté pan or flameproof casserole over medium to medium–high heat. Add the oil and then the bacon lardons and onion. Cook for 3–5 minutes, stirring frequently. Add the beef, sprinkle with flour, and cook for 10 minutes, stirring and turning frequently to brown on all sides.

Add the drained marinade solids from the sieve. Cook, stirring, for 5 minutes, then pour in the marinade. Add enough boiling water to just cover the ingredients. Reduce the heat, cover tightly, and cook over very low heat for at least 3 hours. Toward the end of cooking, taste and adjust the seasonings as desired. Remove from the heat and let cool to room temperature; then refrigerate, covered, preferably until the next day.

Remove and discard the surface fat. Before serving, reheat very gently in a covered pot over low heat, or in a 375°F/190°C oven until heated through.

Add the lardons and onion to the pan and stir for a few minutes until lightly browned, then add to the marinated beef.

Figues rôties à la crème

Pan-roasted figs are combined with caramelized pine nuts in this typical Provence dessert. The sweetness of the figs contrasts nicely with the mild tartness of the crème fraîche.

Preheat the oven to 400°F/200°C. Spread the slivered almonds and pine nuts on a baking sheet. Toast in the oven for 4–5 minutes until golden; watch carefully so they do not burn. Remove from the oven and reserve.

Cut off the stems and pointed tops of the figs. To make the figs look round, shape them gently with your hands.

Melt the butter in a sauté pan over medium heat. Add the figs and sprinkle with a scant 2 tbsp of the sugar. Add ¼ cup of water. Cook for 3–4 minutes, basting the figs a few times with the syrup that forms in the pan. Remove from the heat and set the pan aside in a warm place.

Meanwhile, put the remaining 6 tbsp sugar and 2 tbsp water in a small, heavy saucepan. Stir over a low heat to dissolve the sugar, then increase the heat to medium–high and cook, without stirring, until the mixture bubbles, turns golden, and caramelizes. Take the pan off the heat at once and carefully stir in 2 tbsp warm water (the caramel may splatter).

Place the sauté pan with the figs back over medium heat. Add the toasted almonds and pine nuts and the caramel. Stir in the lemon juice. Bring to a boil, then reduce the heat to medium–low and simmer for 2 minutes. Remove from the heat.

Lightly whisk the crème fraîche to make it airy. Place a few spoonfuls on each plate, top with 3 figs, and spoon the caramel and pine nut sauce over the top. Serve warm.

Serves 6

Preparation 10 minutes
Cooking and finishing
  30 minutes
¼ cup blanched slivered almonds
⅓ cup pine nuts
12 ripe but still firm figs
4 tbsp (½ stick) unsalted butter
½ cup sugar
juice of 1 small lemon
1 cup chilled crème fraîche

Gently press and shape each fig into a ball so they will cook evenly and stand up nicely on the serving plates.

friday

We go behind the scenes in an old-fashioned bakery, then Gui shows us how to make and flavor bread and pastries the Provence way. Find out what Provençal food has in common with the cooking of its nearby neighbor, Italy. Prepare homemade pasta, and discover an easy way to start a meal—with a tempting plate of *charcuterie*.

A la boulangerie

The French describe a sad-looking face as a face looking as long as a day without bread—*une tête longue comme un jour sans pain*. In Provence, as elsewhere in France, a day without fresh bread is very miserable indeed.

Almost invariably, the passion for good fresh bread involves a daily trip to the local bakery—*la boulangerie*. Sometimes this ritual visit takes place twice a day, once in the morning and again in the early evening. French bread dries up quickly and is designed to be eaten on the same day, if not within hours of being baked.

Bakeries keep very long hours. They are the first shops to open in the morning at 7:00 am, or even earlier, and they often stay open until 7:00 or 8:00 pm.

Provence bakeries come in all shapes and sizes. The fancier establishments also double as pastry shops, or *pâtisseries*. This does not mean their bread will taste better—don't make the mistake of judging a bakery by its appearance. The sign of a good bakery is when the shelves are empty by mid-morning.

Behind the scenes

Tucked away, usually in the back of the shop or in the basement, is the room where the dough is made and the bread is baked. As work places go, it's probably not the most comfortable. The heart of the bakery is always very hot because of the ovens, and every surface is covered with a thin coating of flour.

Simple ingredients

Flour, water, yeast, and salt are all the ingredients needed to make a perfect loaf of crusty bread. The ingredients may be simple but the working hours are hard—the process of making dough and baking starts in the middle of the night.

▽

△

Basic tools

The traditional tools of the baker's trade are a long thin rolling pin, a scraper, a saucepan, a bowl, and a well-worn wooden work surface—this is all that an artisan requires.

Baker's skill The recipe is uncomplicated. What makes the difference is the skill of the breadmaker. And what makes a bread unique, and the reason why customers fiercely support one particular bakery over another merely a few doors away, is the baker's personal touch—the way he or she kneads and works the dough. ▽

△
Into the oven Making the dough is the privilege of the master baker. Less experienced hands have the job of putting the dough into the bread tins and then, after resting and rising, of shoving these into the ovens with long-handled wooden peels.

"Learn an old baker's trick: when you're making dough, the easiest way to clean your hands is to rub them with flour. Water just makes them sticky."

Communal baking

Until as recently as the last century in rural Provence, a baker often had the only oven in the village. He rented out oven space, and bakeries played a vital role in village life.

As you like it

Because they like their bread very fresh, many people buy their baguette a half at a time—*une demie*. You can also ask for high-baked bread, *bien cuit*, or not, *pas trop cuit*. And because bakeries are the original "convenience store" of small towns and villages in France, you can buy your morning paper at the same time.

▽

△
Specialty breads

Rapidly gaining popularity, these come in all manner of appealing shapes and sizes— ovals, crowns, sheaves, rolls, and sticks. They are made with subtly different combinations, and are enhanced with raisins, olives, walnuts, or seeds.

"With so many small local bakeries still producing fresh delicious bread, traditionally baked twice a day, it's no surprise that the Provençaux rarely bake at home."

Time and cost Unlike baguettes, which have a price fixed and controlled by the government, speciality breads can be priced by the individual bakers. Some are expensive, such as the sourdough country loaf and the wholemeal loaf below. This reflects the longer time they take to make and the higher cost of ingredients.
▽

△
Morning treats
Even modest *boulangeries* that do not aspire to the status of *pâtisseries* will produce fresh croissants, morning rolls, and simple, appetizing cakes.

Pâte à fougasse

Fougasse is the traditional bread of Provence and a close relative of Italian focaccia. You can flavor this basic fougasse dough with olives, as in the bread recipe on p208, or with herbs, spices, seeds, or bits of cooked bacon.

Makes enough for 4 loaves

Preparation 20 minutes,
  plus rising 2 hours
4 cups bread flour, plus extra for
  dusting
4 cups whole wheat flour
1 tbsp salt
3 envelopes (¼oz each) active
  dried yeast
⅔ cup olive oil

Sift the flours into a mound on a work surface. Use your fist to make a well in the center. Add the salt. In a cup, mix the yeast with ⅔ cup hot tap water. Pour the yeast mixture into the well. Work in a little of the flour. Continue working the ingredients together while you add the oil, a little at a time. Add more water as needed—up to 1 cup—to make a soft paste.

Knead the dough on a lightly floured work surface for 5–6 minutes or until it is smooth and elastic. Put the dough in a large bowl, cover with a clean, damp tea towel or with plastic wrap, and let it rise in a warm, draft-free place for about 1½ hours or until almost doubled in volume.

Uncover the bowl, or turn the risen dough onto a lightly floured surface. Punch down the dough with the side of your hand, then bring back together. Cover again and let rest for 20–30 minutes before using, as directed in the recipe.

Variation
To make the dough using a heavy duty electric mixer equipped with a dough hook, sift the flours into the bowl. With the mixer running on low speed, add the salt and the yeast mixture, then slowly add the olive oil. Increase the speed to medium and knead for 5 minutes.

Pâte à fougasse aux herbes de Provence

After adding the yeast mixture, work in 1 scant tbsp finely chopped fresh thyme or rosemary, or a mixture of herbs chosen from the following: thyme, rosemary, oregano, marjoram, and savory. Thyme and rosemary can be used on their own; the others are more pungent so are best mixed.

Pâte à fougasse à l'anis ou aux graines de fenouil

For anise seed fougasse, add 1 tsp anise seed or 2 tsp pastis (licorice-flavored apéritif) to the dough after working in the yeast. For fennel seed fougasse, add 1 tsp fennel seed.

Fougasse aux olives

Black olives are probably the most popular and traditional way to flavor a fougasse, but the same method can be used with green olives. You can also enhance the basic dough with herbs such as rosemary or thyme.

Makes 4 loaves

Preparation 30 minutes,
 plus making dough and
 rising 30 minutes
Baking 15 minutes
Pâte à Fougasse (p206)
bread flour for dusting
1¼ cups small black olives, pitted
1 medium egg yolk

Divide the dough into 4 equal pieces. Using a rolling pin on a lightly floured surface and working with 1 piece at a time, roll the dough into an oval shape about 8 x 12in (20 x 30cm). Place one-quarter of the black olives on one half of the oval. Brush the other half with water and fold it over to cover the olives. Seal by pressing down the edges with your fingertips. Make a few parallel slashes on the top using the tip of a sharp knife. Repeat with the remaining pieces of dough to make 3 more loaves.

Cover with a dampened clean towel and let rise in a warm place for 30 minutes. The loaves will be ready for baking when the dough feels a little springy when you press it down gently with your thumb.

Preheat the oven to 450°F/230°C. Put the loaves on a large non-stick baking sheet, leaving plenty of room between them. In a cup, mix the egg yolk with 1 tbsp water. Brush the mixture lightly over the loaves. Bake for 15 minutes. Cool on a wire rack for at least 15 minutes before serving.

Fougasse aux lardons

Blanch ¼lb of diced bacon or pancetta in boiling water for 2 minutes. Drain, then sauté with 2 tsp olive oil until crisp. Drain again. Add to the loaves instead of olives.

Fougasse aux anchois

Flavor the dough with herbs (see p206). Finely chop 3 drained anchovy fillets and add to the loaves instead of olives.

Pit the olives, then scatter them over the dough and fold it in half to cover the olives neatly.

Tarte feuilletée à la tomate et à la marjolaine

Puff pastry gives this simple tomato tart with marjoram a rich, buttery edge. You can replace the marjoram with another herb, such as thyme or oregano. Draining and pre-cooking the tomatoes is a crucial step, as it brings out the sweetness of the tomatoes and stops the pastry from becoming soggy.

Serves 4-6

Preparation 45 minutes
Baking 15 minutes

2lb (900g) medium to large,
   vine-ripened tomatoes
fine sea salt and freshly ground
   black pepper to taste
2 tbsp chilled unsalted butter, plus
   soft butter for greasing
1 sheet (about 8oz/225g
) chilled puff pastry
2 tbsp olive oil
1 tbsp chopped fresh marjoram
1 tbsp chopped fresh basil
1 tbsp finely shredded Gruyère
   cheese

Slice the tomatoes thickly and remove some of the seeds and pulp. Put the sliced tomatoes in a colander, sprinkle with a little salt, and let drain for 30 minutes.

Meanwhile, on a lightly-floured surface, roll the puff pastry into a piece about 13in (33cm) in diameter. Generously butter the bottom of a 12in (30cm) tart pan with a removable bottom. Ease the sheet of puff pastry inside the tin, fitting it in loosely. Prick several times with the tines of a fork. Chill for 20 minutes.

Heat the oil in a large frying pan. Lift the tomatoes out of the colander, shaking them to remove excess moisture and pulp, and carefully place in the pan in a single layer. Season with pepper and scatter 1 tsp of marjoram and 1½ tsp basil over the top. Cook over medium–high heat for 3–4 minutes on each side. Transfer to a shallow dish and set aside.

Preheat the oven to 425°F/220°C.

Take the tart pan out of the refrigerator. Press down the pastry to fit it into the pan, and cut off any excess. Prick a few more times around the rim. Sprinkle the pastry with the grated Gruyère and 1 tsp of the marjoram. Next, arrange the tomato slices in concentric circles on top, working toward the center from the outside. Season with pepper and drizzle with the tomato juices left in the dish. Dice the chilled butter into bits and scatter the pieces over the surface.

Bake for 10 minutes. If the tomatoes are browning too quickly, cover loosely with foil. Reduce the heat to 400°F/200°C and bake 5 minutes longer, or until the pastry is crisp and golden brown.

Remove from the oven and let cool on a wire rack before removing the sides of the pan. Scatter the rest of the marjoram and basil over the top of the tart, and serve warm or at room temperature.

Variation
Leftover Tomatoes Provençale (p67) or Ratatouille (p65) make good alternative fillings for this tart. You'll need approximately 2 cups.

Allumettes aux anchois

Always irresistible served piping hot as a party nibble, anchovy and puff pastry cheese straws (*allumettes*, or "matchsticks," in French) also make a good starter alongside a green salad.

Preheat the oven to 425°F/220°C. Put the egg yolk in a bowl and whisk lightly. Remove 2 tsp of it and mix in a cup with 2 tsp water; set this aside for glazing the strips before baking.

Add the crème fraîche to the remaining egg yolk in the bowl, then add 2 tbsp of the Gruyère cheese and the chopped anchovies. Stir to combine and season with a touch of cayenne pepper.

Cut the pastry into 1in (2.5cm) strips. Brush the anchovy mixture over half the strips, then cut all of the strips into 4in (10cm) long rectangles.

Cut a few slashes into the plain pastry rectangles, then lightly place them on top of the anchovy-covered strips. Brush with the egg yolk glaze and sprinkle with the remaining Gruyère.

Put the pastry strips on a non-stick baking sheet. Bake for 10–12 minutes until puffed and golden. Serve hot.

Makes 10-12 straws

Preparation 15 minutes
Baking 10-12 minutes

1 large egg yolk
2 tsp crème fraîche or sour cream
3 tbsp finely shredded Gruyère cheese
4 anchovy fillets in oil, drained and finely chopped
cayenne pepper
1 sheet (about 8oz/225g) chilled puff pastry

"Prepare the allumettes ahead and keep chilled until the oven is piping hot and you are ready to bake."

Pâte brisée

It's always a good idea to make pastry the day before you want to bake a tart, so it has plenty of time to rest and relax. The quantity here makes enough pastry for two 9½in (24cm) tarts.

Put the butter in a small bowl and beat well with a spoon or spatula until it is very soft and creamy—a *pommade*.

Sift the flour onto the work surface and make a well in the center. Add the salt, sugar, and 3 tbsp of cold water into the well and mix in the flour with your fingertips. Add the egg yolk and the softened butter.

Work the ingredients together with your fingertips to make a soft dough. Without kneading it too much, flatten the dough with the palm of your hand against the work surface, then gather it together and flatten it again.

Form the dough into a ball. Line a clean tea towel with flour and wrap the dough in this, then leave to rest in a cool place for at least 2 hours or overnight. The pastry dough can be stored in the refrigerator for 2–3 days or in the freezer for up to 1 month. Allow plenty of time for the dough to return to cool room temperature before using.

Variation

For savory pastry, omit the sugar and increase the salt to 1–1½ tsp.

Makes about 14oz (400g)

Preparation 20 minutes,
  plus resting 2 hours
5 tbsp cold unsalted butter
2 cups flour
½ tsp salt
2 tbsp sugar
1 medium egg yolk

"Beating the butter until it is soft and creamy may be harder work than putting it in the microwave, but it's also easier to control. You want to avoid melting the butter. Once melted, it will never return to its original state."

Tarte aux pignons

Pine nut tart is a traditional festive dessert with a rich ground almond and candied fruit filling topped with delicate pine nuts.

Makes a 9½in (24cm) tart
  to serve 4-6

Preparation 30 minutes,
  plus 4 hours macerating
  and making pastry
Baking 35-40 minutes
½ recipe Pâte Brisée (p213)

For the filling
2 tbsp raisins
3 tbsp rum
5 tbsp soft unsalted butter, plus
  extra for greasing
⅔ cup sugar
about 1⅓ cup (4oz/115g) ground
  almonds
3 small eggs
1 cup diced candied fruit
¾ cup pine nuts

Put the raisins in a cup, add the rum, cover, and set aside to macerate for at least 4 hours or overnight.

Preheat the oven to 400°F/200°C. Generously butter a 9½in (24cm) tart pan with a removable bottom.

In a bowl, mix together the sugar, ground almonds, and soft butter. Beat in the eggs one at a time, then stir in the rum-soaked raisins (along with any remaining rum) and the diced candied fruit.

Roll out the pastry dough thinly on a floured work surface. Lift onto the tart pan and press in lightly with your hands taking care not to stretch the dough. Prick the pastry a few times with the tines of a fork.

Spoon the filling into the pastry and spread evenly with the back of the spoon. Cover the surface with the pine nuts and press in gently. Bake for 35–40 minutes. Let cool completely on a wire rack. Carefully remove the sides of the pan. To serve, cut into wedges.

Scatter the pine nuts evenly over the filling and press them down very gently with your fingertips or the back of a fork.

Panisse

This unprepossessing but—once tasted—quite irresistible chickpea cake is what people used to call poor man's food, and very much in the spirit of the cooking of old Provence.

Serves 6-8

Preparation 45 minutes, plus setting 3 hours
Cooking 3-4 minutes per batch

1 tbsp olive oil
coarse sea salt
soft unsalted butter for greasing
2 cups chickpea flour

To finish

4 tbsp unsalted butter
6 tbsp peanut oil
fine sea salt and freshly ground black pepper to taste

Put 2 cups water, the olive oil, and a generous teaspoon of coarse sea salt in a saucepan and bring to a boil. Meanwhile, butter a 6–7in (16–18cm) long loaf pan.

Sift the chickpea flour into another large saucepan, add 2 cups water, and stir well to mix.

Pour the boiling oiled and salted water into the chickpea flour mixture and whisk well to blend. Set the pan over medium heat and continue whisking until the mixture thickens. Swap the whisk for a wooden spatula and keep on stirring and simmering the thickened, pudding-like chickpea mixture for 10 minutes.

Pour it into the buttered loaf pan. Cover with a damp tea towel and let sit for at least 3 hours until firmly set. (You can cover it with plastic wrap and refrigerate overnight if more convenient.)

Unmold the chickpea cake onto a work surface and cut into ½in (1cm) thick slices.

Heat the butter and oil in a large non-stick frying pan. Working in batches, fry the panisse slices over medium heat for about 2 minutes on each side until golden. Drain on paper towels. Season generously with salt and pepper and serve soon.

"Panisse is great with leftover daube. Also try it as a snack topped with a sprinkling of shredded Gruyère cheese, or alongside a garlicky salad for lunch."

Socca

A typical street food of Nice, these little chickpea cakes look quite plain, but are a remarkably tasty snack to which most people soon become addicted.

Season the chickpea flour with a pinch of salt, a little pepper, the cumin, coriander, and thyme.

Put about 1 cup of water into a medium bowl and add the 3 tbsp olive oil. Stir to blend, then sift in the seasoned flour a little at a time, whisking steadily. Once you have a smooth batter, let it rest at room temperature for at least 1 hour.

Preheat the oven to 450°F/230°C. Generously oil one large or two small non-stick baking sheets. Spread the batter in the sheet(s)to a depth of about ¼in (5mm).

Bake for 25–30 minutes or until golden brown and crisp.

Let cool for a minute, then lift the socca out of the sheet(s). Cut into pieces and serve hot, topped with a drizzling of extra virgin olive oil and, if you like, a grinding of black pepper.

Variation

If you prefer, cook the socca in an oiled crêpe pan or on an oiled griddle, adding the batter a small ladleful at a time. Swirl a little to create a round shape, then cook for about 3 minutes. Turn over and cook for 2 minutes. This is more time-consuming but the socca will be thinner, like a pancake or blini.

Serves 6

Preparation 15 minutes
  plus resting
Baking 25-30 minutes
1 cup chickpea flour
fine sea salt and freshly ground
  black pepper to taste
½ tsp ground cumin
½ tsp ground coriander
½ tsp dried thyme
3 tbsp olive oil, plus extra for
  greasing the baking sheet(s)
extra virgin olive oil for drizzling

Petits gâteaux aux pignons

These golden crescent-shaped cookies are just as easy to make as they are to munch. Ground almonds give a delicate flavor and texture while pine nuts add a luxurious finish.

Makes 16 cookies

Preparation 20 minutes
Baking 8-10 minutes

¾ cup sugar
¼ cup flour
¾ cup ground almonds
1 large egg white
soft unsalted butter or oil
   for greasing
1 large egg
¾ cup pine nuts

Pour 3 tbsp of the sugar into a small, heavy saucepan. Add 2 tbsp water. Stir over medium heat until the sugar has dissolved. Bring to a boil, then simmer for 2 minutes. Remove the syrup from the heat and set aside.

Sift the flour and ground almonds into a bowl. Mix, then add the remaining sugar and mix well. Add the egg white to the bowl. Whisk until you have a smooth, doughy paste.

Preheat the oven to 400°F/200°C. Line one or two baking sheets with parchment paper and grease generously with butter or oil.

Divide the paste in half, and then divide each half into 8 equal portions. Shape each portion into a crescent.

Whisk the whole egg to blend the yolk and white. Spread the pine nuts on a plate. Working one at a time, dip the crescents into the egg, then roll in the pine nuts. Place on the lined baking sheet(s). Bake for 8–10 minutes or until golden and cooked through.

Let the cookies cool on the baking sheet(s) for 2 minutes, then brush with the sugar syrup. Transfer to a wire rack to cool completely before serving. You can store the cookies in an airtight tin for up to 1 week.

Petits sablés à la lavande

Dried lavender flowers may seem to be more at home in the linen closet than in the kitchen cupboard, but their distinctive aromatic sweetness can be put to good culinary use. Use them to flavor cookies, as here, or in stewed, sautéed, or baked apples; poached pears and quinces; or custards.

Makes 16-18 cookies

Preparation 20 minutes,
  plus chilling
Baking 15 minutes
1 stick (4oz) unsalted butter, plus
  extra soft butter for greasing
¼ cup sugar
1 cup flour, plus extra for dusting
1 tbsp cornstarch
1 tbsp ground almonds
1 tsp orange flower water
2 generous tsp dried lavender
  flowers
1 small egg
1 medium egg yolk

Put the butter and sugar into the bowl of a food processor fitted with the metal blade. Process until pale and fluffy. Scrape down the sides of the bowl with a spatula.

Sift in the flour and cornstarch, then add the ground almonds, orange flower water, lavender flowers, and the whole egg. Process, pulsing the machine on and off, until the dough just barely comes together to form a ball.

Remove the dough from the food processor. Dust the dough lightly with flour, wrap in plastic wrap, and refrigerate for 20 minutes.

Preheat the oven to 375°F/190°C. Lightly butter a baking sheet. Dust a cool work surface and a rolling pin with flour.

Place the dough on the floured surface and roll it out to a thickness of about ⅛in (3mm). Stamp out circles of dough with a 2½in (6cm) round cutter. Transfer dough rounds to the baking sheet without crowding.

In a cup, mix the egg yolk with 2 tsp water. Brush this glaze lightly over the dough. Bake for 12 minutes until the cookies are lightly browned at the edges.

Leave cookies in the turned-off oven to firm for 5 minutes, then remove the sheet and cool for 15 minutes. Slide the cookies onto a wire rack and let cool completely before serving. You can store the cookies in an airtight tin for up to 1 week.

"Lavender flowers are good for flavoring granulated confectioners' (powdered) sugar, just like a vanilla bean. They are hard to separate from the sugar, so put them in a piece of muslin and tie securely before you add them to the sugar jar."

Madeleines au miel à la lavande

Lavender honey gives these traditional little cakes a distinctive Provençal flavor. They are the perfect teatime treat. Delicate madeleines are best enjoyed on the same day they are made, although they will keep in an airtight tin for a couple of days.

Preheat the oven to 375°F/190°C. Generously grease the madeleine tins with soft butter.

Sift the flour and salt together. Melt the stick of butter and set aside to cool slightly.

Break the eggs into a bowl. Add the granulated sugar and honey. Whisk with an electric mixer for at least 5 minutes until pale and creamy.

Gently fold in the flour and lemon zest followed by the melted butter, taking care not to deflate the mixture.

Spoon a scant tablespoon of the mixture into each of the buttered madeleine tins. Bake for 7–10 minutes or until puffed and golden brown.

Remove from the oven and immediately unmold onto a wire rack to cool. Dust with confectioners' sugar before serving.

Makes 24 cakes

Preparation 20 minutes
Baking 7-8 minutes
7½ tbsp unsalted butter, plus extra
  soft butter for greasing
¾ cup flour
½ tsp salt
3 medium eggs
¼ cup granulated sugar
3 tbsp lavender honey
grated zest of 1 lemon
sifted confectioners' (powdered)
  sugar for dusting

Whisk the eggs and honey to a frothy cream before adding the flour and melted butter—the mixture should be thick and flow smoothly from the spoon into the tins.

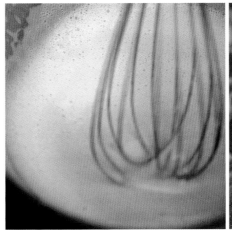

L'influence italienne

Provence was cut off from the rest of France until the coming of the railway, and until the middle of the nineteenth century, great stretches of it, particularly around Nice and its hinterland, were part of the Italian kingdom of Savoy. You can taste the Italian influence in many Provençal dishes.

The culinary tradition of Provence can be described as Mediterranean French, but the flavors and style of the cooking of Italy's Piedmont and Liguria are never far away. Pasta, rice, and gnocchi dishes are very popular. Delicately filled ravioli are served as a starter or light main course, just as in Italy, but in Provence most pasta and rice tend to be served as a side dish rather than as a separate course. For many people, daube, the most Provençal of meat dishes, is not complete without a helping of macaroni on the side. In addition, the traditional Provençal bread, fougasse, is a close cousin of both focaccia and ciabatta.

Basil, garlic, fennel, olive oil, and lemon are flavors equally at home on both sides of the border. Pistou is related to the classic Italian pesto—but it does not include pine nuts. Vegetable and bean soups such as Soupe au Pistou (p73) have much in common with the robust Italian minestrone. Tomatoes, red peppers, zucchini, and eggplants are delicious cornerstones of the cuisine of the area, whether you are eating in Nice or Genoa.

"It's not really surprising that the foods of Provence and Italy have so much in common. If you'll forgive the pun, they happen to share *la même mère* (the same mother)—*la Mer Méditerranée*."

Pissaladière

This classic onion and olive tart is the Provence version of pizza. And, just like its Italian relative, it can be very good or a complete disappointment. Beware of undercooked onions and overly salty anchovies. The secret to success is meltingly tender onions and well-drained, top-quality anchovies.

Serves 8

Preparation 20 minutes,
  plus making pastry
Cooking 1¼ hours
12oz (350g) savory Pâte Brisée
  (p213)
soft unsalted butter for greasing

For the filling
¼ cup olive oil, plus a little extra
  to finish
3lb (1.3kg) large mild onions,
  thinly sliced
4 fresh sage leaves, torn or
  snipped
3 garlic cloves, crushed
fine sea salt and freshly ground
  black pepper to taste
12 anchovy fillets in oil, drained
about 20 small black olives, pitted
  if desired
a few sprigs of fresh thyme
  (optional)

First prepare the pastry shell. Butter a 12in (30cm) tart pan with a removeable bottom. Dust the work surface with flour, then roll out the pastry dough thinly. Lift onto the pan and press in lightly with your hands without stretching the dough. Prick a few times with the tines of a fork. Cover and refrigerate until needed.

Heat the oil in a large frying pan. Add the onions and sage, cover, and cook gently until softened but not browned. Keep the heat very low, occasionally lifting the lid to stir the onions. After 15 minutes add the garlic. Season lightly with salt and generously with pepper. Stir, then cover again and continue cooking. Continue to lift the lid and stir from time to time, always keeping the heat low.

Preheat the oven to 400°F/200°C. Line the pastry with parchment paper or foil and fill with dried beans. Bake for 15–20 minutes until crisp and cooked through. Cool, then remove the beans and paper or foil lining. Leave the oven on.

Meanwhile, continue cooking the onions over low heat, stirring from time to time, until very soft. This will take at least 45 minutes longer.

Spread the onions in the pastry shell. Arrange the anchovy fillets on top and dot with the olives. Sprinkle with a little olive oil and bake for 15 minutes.

Serve hot, warm, or at room temperature. If you like, scatter with a little more sage or thyme just before serving.

Cook the onions as slowly and patiently as you can—they need plenty of time over very low heat if you want them to become meltingly sweet.

Pâte à raviolis fraîche

This pasta dough can be used for the raviolis filled with a spinach, beef, and veal stuffing, (see p233), as well as cannelloni and wide, flat noodles (see below).

Makes about 1lb (450g)

Preparation 20 minutes, plus resting 2 hours

3 cups flour
4 medium eggs

Sift the flour into a mound on the work surface and make a well in the center. Whisk the eggs in a bowl until frothy. Pour the eggs into the well.

Start mixing the eggs slowly into the flour with the fingertips of one hand. Use a dough scraper to push the flour into the eggs.

Continue mixing as the ingredients come together to make a dough. After a while, apply a little more pressure to the dough as you knead it. Continue kneading for 8–10 minutes or until you have a smooth, pliable dough.

Dust a clean tea towel with flour. Form the dough into a ball and wrap in the floured towel. Let rest in the refrigerator for 2 hours.

Cannelloni

Divide the dough into 4 balls. Roll out each ball as thinly as possible, about (¹⁄₁₆in/1-2mm), then cut into 4 rectangles about 4 x 3in (10 x 7.5cm). Let dry on a clean tea towel for 2–3 hours before using.

Nouilles fraîches

Divide the dough into 6 balls. Roll out each ball thinly into a rectangle about 4 x 12in (10 x 30cm). Let rest for 30 minutes without letting the rectangles overlap. Cut with a small, sharp knife into ¼in (5mm) wide strips. Let the noodles dry for at least 2 hours before using.

"There's no need to add salt to the dough, but always remember to be generous when you salt the boiling water for cooking the pasta."

Raviolis maison

Ravioli made by hand will look a little rougher around the edges than store-bought ones, but they are guaranteed to delight your guests. If serving them at once is not possible, refrigerate and cook within 24 hours.

To prepare the filling, cook the spinach until wilted (see p281), then chop it. Set a large frying pan over medium–high heat, add the oil and minced veal, and cook, stirring often, until nicely browned. Season lightly. Add the onions and garlic, then reduce the heat. Cook for 10 minutes, stirring frequently. Add the spinach and cook 10 minutes longer, still stirring. Remove from the heat and stir in the cooked beef. Season again, then set aside to cool. Stir in the eggs until blended.

Divide the pasta dough and the filling into three portions. Roll out one portion of dough on a cold floured work surface into a long, thin strip about 3in (7.5cm) wide. Trim the edges to neaten them, if necessary. Put small balls of filling along the strip of dough, 1in (2.5cm) from the edge and leaving about 1in (2.5cm) between them. Fold the dough over and press down firmly with the side of your hand to seal each ball of stuffing. Separate the ravioli, then put them on a large baking sheet lined with a clean cloth. Repeat with the remaining two portions of dough and filling. Leave the ravioli in a cool place for 2 hours before cooking, or refrigerate longer if convenient.

Bring a large pot of water to a boil. Season with salt. Drop the ravioli, about a dozen at a time, into the simmering water and cook for 3–5 minutes until done. The best way to test is to lift one with a slotted spoon and to taste it. Lift out the cooked ravioli with the slotted spoon, draining carefully, and place in a warmed deep serving dish. Cover to keep warm while you cook the remaining ravioli.

Meanwhile, heat the tomato or daube sauce until piping hot. Spoon the sauce over the ravioli, sprinkle with the grated cheese, and serve at once.

Serves 6-8

Preparation 30 minutes,
  plus making dough and
  resting 2-3 hours
Cooking 15 minutes
Pâte à Raviolis Fraîche (p230)
  all-purpose or bread flour
  for dredging
For the filling
1lb (450g) spinach
¼ cup peanut oil
1lb (450g) ground veal
fine sea salt and freshly ground
  black pepper
2 mild onions, finely chopped
3 garlic cloves, crushed
¼lb (125g) cooked beef or beef
  from Daube (p192), minced
2 medium eggs
To serve
Sauce Tomate Classique (p125) or
  2 cups leftover Daube sauce
about 4oz (115g) Gruyère cheese

Fold over the other long side of the dough strip to cover the balls of stuffing and press to seal, then cut into ravioli with a pastry wheel.

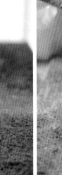

Gnocchi aux épinards

Even if you are a novice at making pasta, these succulent spinach gnocchi take less than 30 minutes to prepare and taste thoroughly good.

Serves 6

Preparation 30 minutes,
 plus resting 1 hour
Cooking 15 minutes
2lb (900g) spinach
2 tbsp unsalted butter
coarse sea salt
3 medium egg yolks
1 cup shredded Gruyère cheese
½ tsp freshly grated nutmeg
2¾ cups bread flour, plus extra
 flour for dredging
fine sea salt and freshly ground
 black pepper to taste

To serve
anchovy butter (see Steak au
 Beurre d'Anchois, p187), melted,
 or Coulis à la Tomate (p124),
 warmed

Rinse the spinach. Put it in a non-stick sauté pan with the butter, sprinkle with a pinch of coarse sea salt, and stir over medium–high heat until wilted. Turn into a colander. Leave for 5 minutes until cool enough to handle, then press firmly with your hands to squeeze out as much moisture as possible. Chop the spinach finely.

In a bowl, mix together the spinach, egg yolks, Gruyère, and nutmeg. Sift in the flour and continue stirring until well mixed. Season generously. Cover and chill for at least 1 hour.

Dredge a cold work surface with flour. Shape the spinach dough into small walnut-sized, shell-shaped gnocchi and roll them gently in the flour on the surface. If you like, keep them on a floured baking sheet in a cool place until ready to cook.

Bring a large pot of water to a boil. Season with salt. Drop the gnocchi into the simmering water and cook gently for about 7 minutes or until done—they will float to the surface once they are ready. Drain carefully in a colander.

Put the gnocchi in a warmed shallow bowl and toss gently with melted anchovy butter or tomato sauce. Serve at once.

"Fresh pasta has to be just that—absolutely fresh. It's not worthwhile making pasta at home unless you are going to use it the same day. These gnocchi can be prepared and enjoyed in minutes."

Riz à l'étouffée

The Provençal description for this rice dish is *à l'estoufado*, which means "smothered." A cousin of risotto, but requiring less constant attention during cooking, this rice with peas and onions makes a very good starter or side dish.

Heat 1 tbsp of the olive oil in a sauté pan and cook the onion over medium heat until softened but not browned. Using a slotted spoon, remove the onion from the pan and set aside.

While the onion is cooking, heat the stock in a saucepan until just simmering.

Heat the rest of the olive oil in the sauté pan, then stir in the rice and saffron. Cook over medium heat, stirring, for 2–3 minutes until the rice is coated in oil and translucent. Pour in the simmering stock and stir once. Reduce the heat, cover, and cook gently for 10 minutes without stirring.

Remove the lid from the sauté pan. Stir the onion into the rice and continue cooking, uncovered and without stirring, for 5 minutes. Stir in the peas and add a little warm water if the rice looks dry and is still a little tough. Continue cooking for 3–4 minutes until the rice is just tender and the grains separate easily.

Remove from the heat. Fluff up the rice with a fork and adjust the seasoning. Transfer to a serving bowl, stir in the butter and parsley, and serve soon.

Serves 4

Preparation 10 minutes
Cooking 20 minutes
3 tbsp olive oil
1 large mild onion, finely chopped
1 cup Camargue (French red rice)
   or brown or white long-grain rice
2 cups chicken or vegetable stock
pinch of saffron strands or powder
1 cup shelled petit peas, thawed
   if frozen
fine sea salt and freshly ground
   black pepper to taste
1 tbsp unsalted butter
1 tbsp finely chopped flat-leaf
   parsley

dinner

Menu

charcuterie,
fondue d'aubergines

polenta à la saucisse
et aux champignons

palets de chocolat
aux noisettes,
glace vanille
au parfum de
basilic

Charcuterie

Charcuterie describes both the pork butcher's shop and the meats sold there. Shops often double up as delis, and cold meats, pâtés, prepared salads, special dishes of the day, and dipping sauces are regular foods to go. An assortment of store-bought cold starters is a tempting and easy way to begin a meal, especially on a mellow Provence evening.

Socca d'Entrevaux (illustrated top left) is dried cured beef, a speciality of the small picturesque town of Entrevaux in the foothills of the Alps, a 40 minutes drive north of Nice. This is Provence's answer to Italian bresaola and Swiss *viande des grisons*. Socca is served in wafer-thin slices with a drizzle of olive oil and, sometimes, with black olives.

Although Provence is not particularly famed for its pork, the rural tradition of slaughtering the pig in winter and making air-dried or cured sausages or salamis that would be ready to eat around Easter, after the fast of Lent, has endured. Local *saucissons* (bottom left) are generously seasoned with herbs and spices. They tend to be fairly dry and sweetly salty. Unless you have a skilled pair of hands and a very sharp knife or a slicing machine, buy them very thinly sliced. Serve with crisp breadsticks, which are known as *gressins* on the Provence side of the border.

Figatelli, smoked and semi-dried aromatic liver sausages (bottom right), are another traditional favorite.

Crunchy radishes, Fondue d'Aubergine (p62), freshly made green and black tapenades (p117), and black olives will complement the spread of *charcuterie*.

"Think antipasti, tapas, and mezze. It's not laziness on the part of the cook to serve *charcuterie*—it's just like buying good bread and fresh hot croissants for breakfast rather than spending half the night baking. You make the most of the skills of specialist artisans."

Polenta

Make sure to read the instructions on the package of polenta. Some polenta is pre-steamed, which speeds up the cooking process. Some is described as "instant" and is quick and convenient, but doesn't produce quite the best taste and texture. Once cooked and set, polenta can be cut into pieces, grilled, and topped with cheese—a delicious accompaniment to sausages (see p242).

Combine 4 cups water, the olive oil, and coarse sea salt in a large sauté pan. Bring to a boil, then gradually add the polenta in a slow, steady stream, stirring well with a wooden spoon to blend.

Stir constantly over medium heat for 12–15 minutes or until the mixture thickens and becomes like a thick porridge. The cooking time will depend on the type of polenta you use; check the instructions on the package.

Remove from the heat and let cool a little, then spoon the polenta onto the center of a clean linen tea towel.

Bring up the four corners of the towel to enclose the polenta, and press down gently to shape it into a round cake about 8in (20cm) in diameter. Set aside to cool for 20 minutes or until firm, then peel away the cloth. Slice or cut the polenta into wedges and use as desired.

Variation
Instead of shaping the polenta into a cake inside a towel, pour it into a lightly buttered loaf pan or round cake pan. Let cool and set before slicing.

Serves 4

Preparation 20 minutes,
  plus resting 20 minutes
Cooking 20 minutes
2 tbsp olive oil
2 tsp coarse sea salt
1½ cups fine-textured polenta or
  yellow cornmeal

"Polenta makes a good and different side dish. Also remember to try it as a base for savory toppings, as a replacement for bread croûtons."

Polenta à la saucisse et aux champignons

Broiled polenta topped with grated cheese makes a perfect base for spicy sausages and mushrooms. Good hearty supper fare for a winter's evening.

Serves 4

Preparation 15 minutes
Cooking 30 minutes
Polenta (p241), cooled and set
⅓ cup shredded Gruyère cheese
4 spicy sausages
12oz (350g) brown (cremini)
    mushrooms
2 tbsp butter
2 tbsp olive oil
fine sea salt and freshly ground
    black pepper to taste
leaves from 4 sprigs of
    flat-leaf parsley, chopped
2 garlic cloves, crushed

Cut the polenta into ½in (1cm) thick slices. Cut the longer slices in half. Lay the slices flat on a baking sheet and sprinkle with the grated cheese. Set aside until ready to use.

Cook the sausages in a ridged cast-iron grill pan over medium heat, turning a few times, for 15–20 minutes or until cooked through.

Meanwhile, wipe the mushrooms clean with damp paper towels, then cut into thick slices. Heat the butter and oil in a large non-stick frying pan. Add the mushrooms, season with salt and pepper, and cook over medium heat, stirring frequently, for about 5 minutes. Stir in the parsley and garlic. Turn up the heat a little and continue cooking for 3–5 minutes. Adjust the seasonings and remove from the heat. Preheat the broiler.

Broil the polenta slices, cheese side up, until bubbly-hot and golden.

Spoon the mushrooms into the center of a large serving dish and put the sausages on top. Surround with the polenta slices and serve at once.

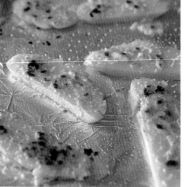

Grilling gives a nice crusty surface to otherwise soft polenta. Lining the baking sheet with foil will help with the clean-up afterward.

Glace vanille au parfum de basilic

Homemade vanilla ice cream is well worth making. Its fresh flavor and slightly grainy texture are quite unlike those of commercially prepared ice creams. To set this apart even further, fresh basil is added for a tantalizing peppery note.

Serves 4

Preparation and cooking
  40 minutes, plus cooling
  and freezing
1¼ cups whole milk
3 vanilla beans, split
4 medium egg yolks
½ cup sugar
½ cup chilled crème fraîche
1 tbsp thinly shredded or chopped
  fresh basil

To serve
tiny sprigs of fresh basil
raspberries (optional)

Put the milk and vanilla beans in a heavy saucepan and bring to a boil over low heat. As soon as the milk starts to bubble around the edges, turn down the heat and simmer gently for 5 minutes longer. Take the pan off the heat and set aside to steep for 30 minutes.

In a large bowl, whisk the egg yolks with the sugar for 3–5 minutes until light and fluffy. Remove the vanilla bean pods from the milk, scraping any remaining seeds from the pods back into the milk using the tip of a sharp knife. Pour the warm milk a little at a time over the egg yolk and sugar mixture, whisking vigorously.

Pour the mixture back into the saucepan and cook over low heat. Bring to a fast simmer, stirring with a large wooden spoon. The custard will thicken gradually until it coats the back of the spoon. Take care not to allow the custard to boil, which would make it curdle. You'll find it helpful to lift the pan off the heat several times during cooking to control the temperature. When thickened, remove from the heat.

Strain through a fine sieve into a bowl. (It's okay for the tiny vanilla seeds to remain in the custard.) Set aside to cool, stirring the custard frequently.

Whisk the chilled crème fraîche until smooth, then fold into the cold custard. Stir in the basil. Pour the mixture into an ice-cream maker and freeze according to the manufacturers' directions. Transfer to a container and freeze until ready to serve.

Remove the ice cream from the freezer about 10 minutes before serving (allow a little longer if the room temperature is cold). Spoon into individual bowls or glasses. Garnish the ice cream with a few tiny sprigs of basil and serve with raspberries, if you like.

Variation
If you're not using an ice-cream maker, pour the mixture into a container and freeze for 45 minutes. Remove the container from the freezer and process the mixture in the food processor for a few seconds. Return to the freezer for 45 minutes, then process the mixture again. Return mixture to the freezer until firm enough to scoop. When made this way, ice cream is best eaten on the same day it is made.

Glace à la vanille

For plain vanilla ice cream, simply omit the basil.

Glace au miel

Omit the basil and replace the sugar with a flower-scented liquid honey. Lavender and acacia honeys are particularly good.

Glace aux raisins secs

In a small saucepan, gently cook 3 tbsp plump dark or golden raisins with 1–2 tbsp rum over low heat for 2 minutes until piping hot. Remove from the heat. Let cool, stirring a few times. Fold the raisins into the vanilla ice cream (above) just before churning or freezing.

"What makes home-churned ice creams worth the effort is their vibrant freshness. Enjoy on the same day they are made or within 48 hours of freezing."

Palets de chocolat aux noisettes

These chocolate and hazelnut wafers are a chocoholic's dream come true. The recipe below makes 20—far more than needed to serve with ice cream for 4 people. Store the remaining wafers in an airtight container in a cool place and enjoy them for up to 5 days.

Toast the chopped hazelnuts in a non-stick frying pan over medium heat for 2 minutes or until lightly browned and fragrant. Remove from the heat and set aside.

Melt the chocolate in the top of a double boiler or in a heatproof bowl placed over (but not touching) barely simmering water. Remove from the heat. Add the oil to the chocolate, whisking constantly. Continue whisking for 5 minutes, occasionally returning the bowl of chocolate to the pan of hot water if necessary to keep it soft enough to whisk.

Remove the chocolate from over the hot water. Stir in the toasted hazelnuts with a wooden spoon to mix well.

Place a sheet of parchment paper on a work surface. Place a scant tablespoon of the chocolate mixture on the paper. Flatten with the back of a fork into a circle that is roughly 2½in (7–8cm) diameter and ⅛in (3mm) thick.

Working quickly, repeat until you have used up all of the chocolate mixture. Keep the water simmering in the bottom of the pan—if the chocolate mixture becomes too hard, return it to the heat for a few seconds until softened enough to spread.

Let the wafers cool and set before serving. If desired, refrigerate for a few minutes until they become firm.

Makes 20 wafers

Preparation 15 minutes,
  plus cooling and setting

1 cup chopped, shelled, and
  skinned hazelnuts (filberts)
9oz (250g) best quality bittersweet
  or semisweet chocolate, chopped
2 tsp peanut oil

Ease the solid chocolate mixture off the spoon with a small fork, then turn the fork over and use the back to flatten each wafer.

saturday

Learn a trick from Gui and his fellow professional chefs, and get to the fish market very early—in time to pick the best of the catch of the day. Find out how to tell if fish and shellfish are truly fresh. Discover how to prepare the fragrant classics of Provençal fish and seafood cookery.

Au marché aux poissons

Fish, glorious fish... the fish markets of Provence display a stunning variety of glistening fresh catches of the day. This is not surprising as the region has a very long, curving coastline stretching from the Rhone delta west of Marseilles to the Italian border to the east. The fishermen of Provence have traditionally worked quite close to the coast, in small boats, leaving from local harbors very early in the morning.

Monday is the only day of the week you won't be able to go to a fish market—fishing boats don't go out to sea on Sunday. The best day to buy fish used to be Friday, when the Catholic church required people to abstain from eating meat. These days, however, many markets are at their shimmering best on the weekend when people are more willing to loosen their purse strings.

Fish prices have soared in Provence, as elsewhere, and fresh fish and seafood are now luxury ingredients. This reflects the sad fact that the bounteous Mediterranean is severely overfished. It's particularly depleted to the east, where the coast is more built up and polluted.

The best and freshest

You must use good-quality fish or your dish will be ruined even before you start cooking. Fish and seafood are much more perishable than meat and poultry. So never buy anything that is not absolutely fresh.

Select
How can you tell that fish is truly fresh? Look for fish that is displayed on a good layer of ice. Even if it was caught locally, earlier that morning, it should be kept chilled at all times.

▽

△
Look and feel
The eyes should be bright and rounded, with dark pupils and transparent corneas. If you press the side of the fish with your fingers, it should be soft but not squishy and should spring back quickly without leaving a mark.

Check carefully

Always take a close look at the gills. Lift them gently if possible. They should be bright pinky red and full—they will start looking dark and dirty as the fish ages.

▽

△

Smell

Choosing fish really comes down to common sense. Fresh fish always looks unmistakably bright and shiny—it should be clean and almost appetizing on its bed of ice. Remember never to buy anything that has the faintest whiff of staleness, brine, or ammonia.

"Beware of fishy smells… genuinely fresh fish has a clean, light aroma. Don't be shy, have a good sniff. If it smells even very faintly unpleasant, don't buy it."

Dazzingly different

Many varieties of fish are still found in the Mediterranean. Some are unfamiliar—even to visitors from other parts of France. Varieties also seem to change slightly from harbor to harbor and market to market, with names having local variations.

Ultra-fresh

Top-quality fish and seafood sell very quickly and at a high price. So the rules are to get to the market very early—preferably around 8:00 am and certainly no later than 9:00 am—and be prepared to pay for the best.

△
Seasonal specialty

Some fishy treats are as short lived as they are local. Silvery *poutine*, tiny baby anchovies, are only available along small stretches of the coast for 2 weeks in the early spring. They are delicious served on thick slices of garlicky toast.

Buy local   Much of the pleasure ▷
of shopping along the coast of Provence for
the day's catch comes from not knowing in
advance what's going to be available. Will
there be sea bream or daurade, or will it be
loup de mer (bass) or *rouget* (red mullet)?
Whatever the fish, look out for the words
pêche locale—locally fished.

△
Flavorings for free   One of
the perks of buying fish at a market is that very
often you are offered a free sprig or bunch of
parsley to use in cooking. Some fishmongers
will also sell fresh lemons, but in Provence they
assume that you already have the last essential
flavoring—a few cloves of garlic.

"Provence is not the place to
play it safe when cooking with
fish. Be adventurous and use
the varieties available to try
new recipes."

Preparing mussels

Just like other fish and seafood, mussels should never be stored in their original wrapping. So the moment you get home, rinse them well, then keep them in a large bowl, covered with a damp towel, in the bottom of the refrigerator for up to 24 hours. Mussels are usually cooked, but very fresh mussels can be eaten raw, just like oysters.

Rinse   Remove the mussels from their bag and put a handful at a time into a colander. Rinse under cold running water, scrubbing with a brush if the shells look gritty.

Debeard   Pull out the "beards." Any mussels that stay open after cleaning or look half-opened may be dead. Put a little pressure on the shell with your fingers; if the mussel doesn't react, throw it away.

Fumet de moules

The stock from cooking mussels—a combination of wine, aromatics, and the liquor from the mussels—is delicious and useful for many seafood dishes, most famously the popular Moules Marinières (see recipe p260).

Makes about 1½ cups

Preparation and cooking
  20 minutes

5lb (2.3kg) fresh mussels
6 stalks dried fennel about
   4in (10cm) long, or 3 stalks
   fresh fennel
2 bay leaves
2in (5cm) piece dried orange peel
   (see pp328–329)
3 large or 12 small shallots,
   finely chopped
1 cup dry white wine
freshly ground black pepper
   to taste

Rinse and debeard the mussels (see p257). Turn them into a large saucepan or Dutch oven. Add the fennel, bay leaves, orange peel, and shallots. Pour in the wine.

Bring to a boil over high heat, then cover the pan and cook for 5–6 minutes until the mussel shells open. Without lifting the lid, shake the pan a few times during cooking to move the mussels around.

Remove the saucepan from the heat. Lift out the mussels with a slotted spoon and reserve for whichever recipe you've chosen. (Spoon 2–3 tbsp of the strained mussel stock over them to keep them moist, then let cool slightly and refrigerate for up to 24 hours.)

Let the cooking liquid cool for 2–3 minutes. Hold a chinois or sieve lined with unbleached muslin or a double-thickness of cheesecloth over a saucepan (if using the stock immediately) or a bowl. Strain the liquid through the sieve without pressing through any gritty sediment. Adjust the seasonings before using. The stock can be refrigerated, covered, for up to 48 hours or frozen. Bring back to a boil before using.

Fumet de clovisses

Substitute clams for the mussels. Wash the clams very thoroughly at least twice in a large pan of cold water. Cook with the wine and flavorings, uncovered, for 7–8 minutes, stirring frequently, or until the clams open. Lift out with a slotted spoon and drain in a colander placed over a bowl. Strain the cooking liquid through a sieve lined with a double layer of muslin or cheesecloth, without pressing through any of the gritty sediment. The stock can be refrigerated, covered, for up to 48 hours or frozen. Bring to a boil and adjust the seasonings before using. This makes a very good stock for cooking pasta and rice. Add the shelled clams to the dish (see Pilaf de Moules au Safran, p266). Or, serve the clams grilled on the half shell (2 clams in each half shell) topped with a savory butter (see pp132–133).

Moules marinières de Provence

Liberal amounts of fennel, garlic, shallots, and parsley make this traditional mussel dish particularly aromatic. Some purists argue that cream should not be used for classic *marinière* mussels, but it does add a smooth finishing touch.

Serves 4-5

Preparation 15 minutes,
 plus steaming mussels
Cooking 15 minutes

5lb (2.3kg) fresh mussels, steamed
 open, and about 1½ cups
 Fumet de Moules (p258)
3 tbsp unsalted butter
3 large shallots, finely chopped
4 garlic cloves, finely chopped
leaves from 4 sprigs of
 flat-leaf parsley
2 stalks dried fennel about 4in
 (10cm) long, broken up
1 cup dry white wine
1 cup light cream or half-and-half,
 or more if needed
freshly ground black pepper
 to taste
1 tsp white wine vinegar

Prepare the mussels and mussel stock as directed on pp257–258.

Melt the butter in a large sauté pan or Dutch oven over medium heat. Add the shallots, reduce the heat a little, and cook for 2–3 minutes, stirring occasionally, until softened. Add the garlic, parsley, and fennel, and stir for 30 seconds.

Increase the heat to medium. Pour in the wine and bring to a simmer. Add 1 cup of the mussel stock. Return to a simmer and cook gently for 3–4 minutes. Stir in the cream and season with pepper. Bring just to a simmer; then remove from the heat.

Discard the fennel stalks. Taste and adjust the seasonings—this is the best time to adjust the flavor of the sauce. Add a little more cream if it's too salty; if it's too bland, add more mussel stock. Set aside until ready to serve.

About 5 minutes before serving, put the mussels and their juices in a large sauté pan over medium heat. Pour in the sauce and heat through, stirring a few times. At the last minute, stir in the vinegar. Serve at once, directly from the pan or in a tureen.

Cook the flavoring ingredients in butter before adding white wine, mussel stock, and cream to make a luscious sauce for the mussels.

Moules au pastis

Mussels with a pastis and tomato broth flavored with coriander makes a perfect starter. For a main course, serve with boiled and peeled floury potatoes, such as russets, crushed with a little olive oil. If you like, snap off and discard the top shells of the mussels before adding them to the broth.

Serves 4-5

Preparation 20 minutes,
  plus steaming mussels
Cooking 15 minutes

5lb (2.3kg) fresh mussels, steamed
  open, and about 1½ cups
  Fumet de Moules (p258)
2 medium tomatoes
3 tbsp unsalted butter
1 large or 3 small shallots,
  finely chopped
4 garlic cloves, finely chopped
2 tsp whole coriander seeds
6 tbsp pastis (licorice-flavored
  apéritif)
freshly ground black pepper
  to taste
leaves from 3–4 sprigs of cilantro
  (coriander)

Prepare the mussels and mussel stock as directed on pp257–258. Blanch and skin the tomatoes (see p90); remove the seeds and chop the flesh.

Melt the butter in a sauté pan or Dutch oven over medium heat. Add the shallots, garlic, and coriander seeds, reduce the heat a little, and cook, stirring occasionally, for 2–3 minutes. Stir in the chopped tomatoes, then the pastis. Cook, stirring, for 30 seconds.

Increase the heat to medium. Pour in the mussel stock. Bring to a simmer and cook gently for 5 minutes. Season with pepper.

Add the cooked mussels with their juices. Stir over medium heat until piping hot. Scatter with cilantro leaves just before serving.

Variation
Replace the pastis with ½ cup dry vermouth, such as Noilly Prat.

"To turn this dish into a lovely main course, place chopped boiled and peeled floury potatoes in the warmed serving bowls before adding the mussels and their scented broth."

Salade Antibes

This prawn, mussel, and potato salad makes a good dish for a summer buffet, either as a main dish or to serve 6-8 as a starter. You can prepare and cook all the ingredients ahead, then assemble the salad just before serving.

Rinse and debeard the mussels (see p257). Put them in a large sauté pan or Dutch oven, cover tightly, and cook over high heat for 3–5 minutes or until they open. Drain in a colander set over a bowl. Let sit for a few minutes until cool enough to handle, then discard the shells and reserve the mussels in a bowl. Strain the cooking juices through a sieve lined with unbleached muslin or a double-thickness of cheesecloth. Spoon some of the juices over the mussels to keep them moist.

Cook the potatoes in boiling water until tender; drain well. When cool enough to handle, peel and cut into thick slices. Put them in a bowl, add 2 tbsp of the juices from the mussels, and stir gently to coat. Stir in the fennel.

While the potatoes are cooking, put the tomatoes in a colander, season with a little salt, stir, and let drain in the sink or over a bowl. Peel and devein the prawns and remove the heads, but leave on the last section of the tail. Separate the lettuce leaves. Rinse, drain, and dry in a salad spinner.

To make the dressing, finely chop together the garlic and parsley. Scrape into a small liquid measuring cup and add the anchovy, mustard, and shallot. Mash well together with a fork. Beat in the olive oil and vinegar, and season to taste. You can also add any leftover mussel juices, if desired.

To assemble the salad, arrange the drained tomatoes in a large, shallow bowl, then add the potatoes and fennel. Tear or chop the lettuce into bite-size pieces and scatter over the top. Add half the dressing and toss gently. Distribute the mussels on top. Shell the eggs and quarter lengthwise, then tuck into the salad. Arrange the prawns on top and scatter with the olives. Drizzle with the remaining dressing. Snip the chives over the top and season with extra pepper. Keep the salad cool, and serve within 30 minutes.

Serves 4

Preparation and cooking
  45 minutes

2lb (900g) fresh mussels
4 medium to large new potatoes
½ small fennel bulb, chopped
3 medium to large, vine-ripened
  tomatoes, thinly sliced
fine sea salt and freshly ground
  black pepper to taste
8 large tiger prawns, cooked
1 head romaine lettuce
4 medium eggs, hard-boiled
2 tbsp small black olives, pitted
small handful of fresh chives

For the dressing
1 garlic clove, smashed
leaves from 1 sprig of
  flat-leaf parsley
1 small anchovy fillet in oil,
  drained
1 tsp Dijon mustard
1 small shallot, finely chopped
6 tbsp olive oil
1 tbsp red wine vinegar

Pilaf de moules au safran

Rice with mussels and saffron makes an impressive main course. Halfway between paella and risotto, Middle Eastern-inspired pilaf is easy to make and can be prepared a little ahead of the meal. To do this: once the rice is al dente, cover loosely with foil. Keep the rice warm and the remaining stock hot. Just before serving, reheat the rice gently, moisten with a little stock, and add the saffron butter and finishing touches.

Serves 6

Preparation and cooking
  1 hour

4–5lb (1.8–2.3kg) mussels
2 cups dry white wine
3 tbsp olive oil
2 large or 6 small shallots, very
  finely chopped
3 garlic cloves, very finely
  chopped
leaves from 6 sprigs of flat-leaf
  parsley, finely chopped
1½ cups Camargue (French
  red rice) or brown or white
  long-grain rice
fine sea salt and freshly ground
  black pepper to taste
finely grated zest of 1 small lemon

For the saffron butter
2 generous pinches of saffron
  strands or powder
½ stick (2oz) soft unsalted butter

First prepare the saffron butter. Cover the saffron with 3 tbsp hot water and let sit for 5 minutes to soften. Using a fork, mash the saffron mixture well into the butter. Set aside.

Rinse and debeard the mussels (see p257). Turn the mussels into a large saucepan or Dutch oven and add the wine. Cover the pan, set over high heat, and cook for 5–6 minutes until the mussels open (discard any that remain closed). Without lifting the lid, shake the pan a few times during cooking.

Remove from the heat. Lift out the mussels with a slotted spoon and put them in a bowl; reserve. Let the cooking liquid cool for 2–3 minutes, then strain it into a bowl through a sieve lined with unbleached muslin or a double-thickness of cheesecloth. Add 2 cups of just-boiled water to the cooking liquid. Set this mussel stock aside and keep hot.

Heat the oil in a paella pan or sauté pan. Add the shallots and cook over low heat for 2–3 minutes, stirring occasionally, until softened. Add the garlic. Reserve 2 tbsp of the parsley for garnish and add the rest to the pan; stir for 30 seconds. Add the rice and cook, stirring, for 2–3 minutes or until translucent and coated with oil.

Turn up the heat a little. Pour in half of the hot mussel stock. Stir and bring to a simmer. Cook gently for about 10 minutes, stirring from time to time. Add a ladleful of the remaining stock, then stir and cook for another 8–10 minutes or until the rice is tender but still has a little bite to it—taste it to check. Keep the rest of the stock hot and add a few more small ladlefuls during cooking if the rice starts to look dry but still tastes hard. (Any leftover stock can be refrigerated for a day or frozen.)

Reduce the heat to very low. Stir the saffron butter into the rice. Scatter the mussels over the top and tuck some of them into the rice. Cover with foil and cook over very low heat until the mussels are heated through. Adjust the seasonings. Just beore serving, scatter the lemon zest and reserved chopped parsley over the top.

Variation
Add ½lb (225g) cooked peeled prawns to the rice at the same time as the mussels.

Soupe de poissons

Fish soup full of Mediterranean flavors really needs no accompaniment, except perhaps some toasted crusty bread rubbed with garlic. For added flavor and interest, serve with shredded Gruyère cheese and the classic hot pepper and saffron mayonnaise, rouille (p118). Before eating, take a moment to enjoy all of the heady aromas—a good fish soup is deliciously fragrant.

Put the oil in a large, heavy saucepan or Dutch oven. Add the onions and leeks, and cook over medium heat until softened and just golden.

Add the fish and seafood to the pan and stir, then add the fennel, tomatoes, garlic, parsley, bay leaves, orange peel, and tomato paste. Cook, stirring occasionally, for 8–10 minutes or until the fish is just beginning to flake when pierced with a fork. Pour in 10 cups hot water and season lightly. Reduce the heat to low and simmer gently for 20 minutes.

Remove from the heat and let cool a little, stirring and mashing down the soft fish pieces with the back of a large wooden spoon. Remove the fennel, orange peel, and bay leaves. If you like, working in batches, process the soup to a coarse paste in the food processor. Strain the soup through a chinois or a very fine sieve into a clean saucepan. Return the soup to a simmer over medium heat.

Soften the saffron in a ladleful of the soup, then stir into the rest of the soup. Adjust the seasonings. Ladle the soup into bowls. Serve hot, with garlic toasts.

Variation

Try the thrifty Provence custom of adding pieces of spaghetti toward the end of cooking. Break 2oz (60g) of dry spaghetti into ¾in (2cm) pieces and add to the soup after it has been sieved. Simmer for 10 minutes, then add the saffron.

Serves 6

Preparation 20 minutes
Cooking 1 hour

5 tbsp olive oil

4 medium onions, chopped

2 leeks, chopped

3½–4½lb (1.5–2kg) assorted fish and seafood, cleaned and rinsed

4 pieces dried fennel stalks 2in (5cm) long

4 ripe medium tomatoes, quartered

9 garlic cloves, crushed

5 sprigs of fresh flat-leaf parsley

3 bay leaves

6in (15cm) strip dried orange peel (see pp328–329)

1 tbsp tomato paste

fine sea salt and freshly ground black pepper to taste

pinch of saffron strands or powder

To serve
garlic toasts (see p46)

Flavoring is key to the success of this soup, so use a good variety of very fresh fish. Enhance the color with an infusion of golden saffron.

Soupe de moules au fenouil

A typical Provence concoction, this mussel and fennel soup harmoniously combines seafood and vegetables with an aromatic broth.

Serves 4

Preparation and cooking
  1 hour

2lb (900g) fresh mussels

2 cups dry white wine

4 ripe, medium tomatoes

3 tbsp olive oil

1 leek, chopped

2 sprigs each of flat-leaf parsley
   and thyme

1 bay leaf

¼ small fennel bulb, chopped

2in (5cm) piece dried orange peel
   (see pp328–329)

fine sea salt and freshly ground
   black pepper to taste

1 large floury potato such as
   russet, peeled and chopped

pinch of saffron strands

Rinse and debeard the mussels (see p257). Turn them into a large saucepan or Dutch oven. Add the wine, cover the pan, and cook over high heat for 5–6 minutes, or until the mussels open (discard any that remain closed). Without lifting the lid, shake the pan a few times during cooking.

Remove from the heat. Line a sieve with unbleached muslin or a double layer of cheesecloth and place over a bowl. Turn the mussels into the sieve and let drain until cool enough to handle. Remove and discard the shells. Reserve both the mussels and the strained cooking liquid.

Blanch and skin the tomatoes (see p90); remove the seeds and chop the flesh. Heat the olive oil in a large sauté pan over medium heat. Add the tomatoes, leek, parsley, thyme, bay leaf, fennel, and orange peel. Season with salt and pepper. Cook, stirring frequently, until softened.

Add the mussel cooking liquid to the pan, then 2 cups of just-boiled water. Bring to a simmer. Add the potatoes and cook until soft.

Remove from the heat. Let cool a little, then remove the herbs and the orange peel. Mash the potato pieces to thicken the soup.

Soften the saffron strands in a spoonful of the soup and then stir into the rest of the soup. Adjust the seasoning and stir in the mussels. Reheat gently until the mussels are heated through. Serve soon.

Variation

Add 2 tbsp dry spaghetti broken into 1in pieces or 2 tbsp short-grain rice to the soup after you've mashed in the potatoes. Cook gently for 10–12 minutes until tender, then add the saffron mixture and the mussels.

Langoustines à la poêle

You'll need your fingers, a nutcracker, and metal skewers to eat this delicious yet simple dish of pan-fried langoustines. Live langoustines are best kept in the refrigerator until the last minute before cooking. If you prefer, you can substitute uncooked large prawns and reduce the cooking time by 1 minute per side. Cooked langoustines, crayfish, or prawns can of course also be used, reducing the cooking time by half.

Heat half the oil and butter in a large frying pan. Add the langoustines, cover, and cook over high heat for 3 minutes. Remove the lid, turn the langoustines over, and continue cooking for 3 minutes until they have turned a bright pink-orange.

Pour in the brandy, ignite carefully, and cook until the flames die down. Remove the langoustines from the pan and set aside in a warm place—they don't need to be eaten hot.

Add the remaining oil to the pan, then add the scallions and garlic. Cook for a minute over medium heat, stirring, then add the wine. Turn up the heat a little, season, and cook for 3–5 minutes until bubbling hot and slightly reduced.

Meanwhile, if you like, shell the langoustines. If you prefer to let your guest(s) do the shelling, provide the necessary equipment (a nutcracker and metal skewers or small forks), as well as finger bowls and paper napkins.

Remove the pan from the heat. Stir in the parsley and the remaining butter. Serve the sauce piping hot with the warm langoustines.

Serves 2 as a main course,
4 as a starter

Preparation 10 minutes
Cooking 20 minutes
¼ cup olive oil
3 tbsp unsalted butter
8–12 plump, live langoustines
¼ cup brandy
2 large scallions (green onions),
    both white and green parts,
    finely chopped
3 garlic cloves, crushed
½ cup dry white wine
fine sea salt and freshly ground
    black pepper to taste
2 tbsp finely chopped
    flat-leaf parsley

"Langoustine shells make the most fragrant light broth—perfect for cooking rice and pasta or adding to soups and sauces. Cover the shells with simmering water and cook gently for 10 minutes, then cool and strain."

Bouillabaisse

Bouillabaisse is the great rival of Soupe de Poissons as the favorite fish soup of Provence. More of a stew than a soup, this richly aromatic concoction humbly started life as a mixture of unsold "catch of the day" boiled up with vegetables by fishermen. The mix of fish should ideally include a piece of pre-soaked salt cod and another strong flavored fish, such as mackarel or hake.

Serves 4–6

Preparation 20 minutes,
  plus marinating
Cooking 20 minutes

1lb (450g) fresh mussels
3lb (1.3kg) mixed filleted or
  skinless fish (see above)
4 medium tomatoes
6 tbsp olive oil
1 large mild onion, finely chopped
2 small shallots, finely chopped
fine sea salt and freshly ground
  black pepper to taste
cayenne pepper
½ small fennel bulb, finely
  chopped
2 tsp fennel seeds
4 garlic cloves, crushed
5 sprigs of flat-leaf parsley
4 sprigs of thyme
1 bay leaf
4in (10cm) strip of dried orange
  peel (see pp328–329)
generous pinch of saffron
1¼ cups dry white wine
2½ cups Fumet de Moules (p258)
1 tbsp finely chopped flat-leaf
  parsley to garnish

To serve

6 small to medium potatoes,
  peeled and boiled
Aïoli (p131)
1 baguette, split and lightly
  toasted, then rubbed with garlic

Rinse and debeard the mussels (see p257). Cut the fish into 2in (5cm) chunks. Blanch and skin the tomatoes (see p90); remove the seeds and chop the flesh.

In a large, heavy saucepan, heat 2 tbsp of the oil. Add the onion, shallots, and tomatoes. Season lightly and add a little cayenne pepper. Cook over medium heat for 5–6 minutes, stirring a few times. Add the fennel, fennel seeds, garlic, parsley, thyme, bay leaf, and orange peel, then sprinkle in half the saffron. Stir. Reduce the heat and cook for 5 minutes, stirring occasionally.

Remove from the heat. Let cool for 5 minutes, then remove the herbs, bay leaf, and orange peel. Stir in the mussels and place the fish on top. Drizzle with the rest of the olive oil and sprinkle with the rest of the saffron. Stir gently once or twice. Cover and let marinate in a cool place for at least 1 hour.

About 30 minutes before you intend to eat, pour the white wine and mussel stock over the fish mixture. Add just enough cold water to cover the ingredients. Season lightly. Bring to a simmer over medium heat. Reduce the heat a little and simmer for 6–8 minutes until the fish begins to flake.

Using a slotted spoon, transfer the fish and mussels to a warmed shallow serving bowl. Strain the soup through a sieve into a warmed tureen or large jug. Moisten the fish and mussels with a few tablespoons of the soup. Sprinkle the soup with the chopped parsley.

To serve, have a heated soup plate or bowl for each guest, and some spare bowls for discarded mussel shells and fish debris. Put a boiled potato in each bowl, crush gently with a fork, and smear with a little aïoli. Add the fish and mussels, then ladle over plenty of soup. Dig in with a spoon, and also use your fingers and garlic toasts to enjoy bouillabaisse to the fullest.

Loup de mer au fenouil

Grilled sea bass with fennel is a simply sumptuous Provence favorite. Serve with Tomates Provençale (p67) and with the potatoes from the Daurade au Vin Blanc recipe (p276) or a garlicky olive oil mash (see p195).

Serves 4

Preparation 10 minutes
Cooking 30 minutes
1 sea bass, about 2¾lb (1.25kg),
    cleaned
fine sea salt and freshly ground
    black pepper to taste
1 lemon
1 orange
2 stalks dried fennel about
    4in (10cm) long, or 1 stalk
    fresh fennel
¼ cup olive oil
2 tsp ground fennel seeds
3 tbsp soft unsalted butter

Preheat the grill to until very hot. Alternatively, preheat the oven to 425°F/220°C.

Rinse the fish well and pat dry with a clean tea towel or paper towels. Season the inside with salt and pepper. Cut 4 thin slices from the lemon and the orange. Put the slices and the fennel stalks inside the fish. Season the outside. In a small cup, combine the olive oil and ground fennel. Brush all over the fish.

Grill the fish for about 10 minutes on each side, checking the first side after 7–8 minutes of cooking—the skin should be crisp and the flesh inside just flaking a little when tested with a fork. Brush with the flavored oil; then turn and brush the other side.

If cooking in the oven, roast for about 20 minutes. After 12 minutes, take the fish out of the oven, turn it over, and brush again with oil. Return to the oven for another 6–8 minutes, then test with a fork; if the flesh isn't flaking, reduce the heat and continue roasting for 3–5 minutes.

Whether you grill or roast, keep checking the sea bass toward the end of cooking—a couple of minutes can make all the difference.

Meanwhile, squeeze the juice from the rest of the lemon and orange. Melt the butter with the juice in a small saucepan. Stir in 2 tbsp hot water and season with salt and pepper.

Remove the fennel and the orange and lemon slices from inside the fish. Serve at once, with the citrus butter sauce. The crisp skin will come off easily when lifted with a fork, as will the central spine and bones.

Rougets à la tapenade

Red mullet has a sweetly meaty flesh with a delicate taste and texture, so it cooks in a minute and should be flavored sparingly. Tapenade is a good choice for flavoring, but you can replace it with a savory butter, such as parsley or anchovy (see p132). Whole sardines, sea bass fillets, or whole small farmed sea bass can be cooked in the same way.

Rinse the fillets and pat them dry. Heat 2 tbsp of the olive oil in each of 2 non-stick frying pans. Spread the tapenade over the skin side of the fillets and place them in the pan, skin side down. Cook over medium heat for 1 minute. Turn them over carefully and cook for 1–2 minutes longer until the fillets are firm to the touch and just barely cooked through.

Remove from the heat at once, season the fillets with pepper, and serve soon, with wedges of lemon.

Serves 4

Preparation 10 minutes
Cooking 5 minutes

4 medium red mullets, whole
   sardines, sea bass fillets, or
   whole small formed sea bass,
   scaled and filleted
¼ cup olive oil
4 tsp Tapenade Verte (p117)
freshly ground black pepper
   to taste
1 lemon, cut into 4 wedges

"Pan-frying is a good way to cook fish fillets or whole small to medium-sized Mediterranean fish. It's a gentler method and easier to control (in all climates) than cooking on a grill or in the hearth."

Daurade au vin blanc

Sea bream is a much prized Mediterranean fish. It comes in many sizes—as a rule, the larger fish has more flavor. Here it is moistened with white wine, generously flavored with aromatic herbs, and roasted in the oven.

Serves 4

Preparation 20 minutes
Cooking 1 hour

¼ cup olive oil, plus extra for
  greasing
2 large shallots, chopped
2 tomatoes, sliced
6 garlic cloves, sliced
6 sprigs of flat-leaf parsley,
  finely chopped
4 stalks dried (or 2 stalks fresh)
  fennel, about 4in (10cm) long
2 bay leaves
1 lemon, thinly sliced
12 black peppercorns
2 sea bream (porgy), each about
  1¾lb (800g)
1 cup dry white wine
fine sea salt and freshly ground
  black pepper to taste
3 tbsp chilled unsalted butter,
  diced
about 1lb (450g) waxy potatoes,
  peeled and diced
lemon wedges to serve

Preheat the oven to 400°F/200°C. Use olive oil to grease a gratin dish that will hold all the ingredients comfortably. Spread half of the shallots, tomatoes, garlic, parsley, fennel, bay leaves, lemon slices, and peppercorns in the dish. Place the fish on top and put a few lemon slices inside each one. Cover with the rest of the shallots, tomatoes, garlic, parsley, fennel, bay leaves, peppercorns, and lemon slices. Mix the wine with 1 cup of water and pour into the dish. Season with salt and pepper. Scatter the butter over the top. Bake for about 50 minutes.

About 10 minutes after putting the fish in the oven, spread the diced potatoes in another oiled gratin dish. Season with salt and pepper and drizzle with the olive oil. Cover loosely with foil and place in the oven to cook along with the fish. After 20 minutes, remove the dish of potatoes from the oven and stir. Return to the oven.

After 15–20 minutes longer, take both dishes out of the oven. Check that the fish is flaking a little when pierced with a fork and that the potatoes are tender. Scrape the herbs from the fish, leaving the tomato and lemon slices on top, then lift the fish onto a warmed serving dish. Spoon the potatoes around the fish. Keep hot.

Discard the lemon slices and bay leaves. Pour the cooking juices and vegetables into a saucepan and bring to a boil. Cook for 3 minutes, mashing to extract as much liquid from the flavorings as possible. Strain through a chinois or very fine sieve into a small heated pitcher or sauceboat. Taste and adjust the seasonings. Spoon a little sauce over the fish and serve with the remaining sauce and lemon wedges.

Dried fennel, garlic, bay, and lemon add a special Provençal aroma to these delicately flavored fish.

Brandade de morue

This classic purée of salt cod has a distinctive strong and somewhat briny flavor, and may be a bit of a challenge to the palate of people who haven't tasted salt cod before. A good way to initiate beginners is to spread it on small baked croûtons and serve as an appetizer.

Serves 4

Preparation and cooking
 45 minutes, plus soaking
1¾lb (800g) salt cod
3 garlic cloves, crushed
freshly ground black pepper
 to taste
¾ cup olive oil, plus ¼ cup to finish
¾ cup milk
1 floury medium potato (such as
 russet), boiled in its skin, peeled,
 and crushed (optional)
3–4 tbsp light cream or half-and-
 half (optional)
juice of ½ lemon
garlic toasts to serve (see p46)

Rinse the cod well, then place on a trivet. Put into the sink or a large bowl and completely immerse in cold water. Let it soak for about 3 hours, then drain and rinse. Soak the cod in fresh water for another 3 hours. Repeat this soaking process twice until the fish loses the excess curing salt—this can take up to 30 hours if the fish is very salty.

Drain and rinse the cod a final time, then place in a saucepan and cover with fresh cold water. Bring to a simmer over medium heat. Reduce the heat a little and cook the fish gently for 6–8 minutes or until you can flake it easily with a fork.

Remove from the pan, rinse, and drain well. When cool enough to handle, discard the skin and as many bones as you can. Put the fish in a bowl and scatter the garlic over the top. Shred the fish finely with a fork, mashing and combining it with the garlic. Season with pepper.

Rinse out the saucepan and pour in about one-third of the olive oil. Place over very low heat. In a separate pan, gently heat the milk. Take the pan with the olive oil off the heat and add the shredded salt cod. Using a large fork, wooden spoon, or spatula, beat and pound together to blend well.

Return the pan to low heat and continue pounding. Gradually trickle in the remaining olive oil and the warm milk, beating vigorously and constantly. Once you've patiently worked in all the olive oil and milk, the brandade will be a slightly sticky, creamy white purée. If it is too runny—or if you would prefer a milder flavor—beat in the cooked potato, a little at a time. Keep the heat low throughout.

Whisk in the remaining olive oil, the cream, if using, and the lemon juice. Season generously with pepper. Serve piping hot, with garlic toasts.

Thon à la provençale

Tuna with tomato and herbs is a quick and easy main course. You can cook the tomatoes several hours ahead and reheat them while you cook the tuna. Serve with potatoes mashed with garlic and olive oil (see p195).

Thickly slice the tomatoes and remove some of the seeds and pulp. Put the sliced tomatoes in a colander, sprinkle with a little salt, and let drain for 30 minutes.

Heat 3 tbsp of the oil in a sauté pan. Shake the tomatoes as you lift them out of the colander to remove excess moisture and pulp. Season them with pepper, then add them to the hot oil. Add the scallions, garlic, thyme, and half the basil. Cook over medium heat, stirring a few times, for about 8 minutes or until soft. Add the olives and remove from the heat.

Brush the tuna steaks with the remaining olive oil and season with salt and pepper.

Heat a non-stick griddle or frying pan. Once the pan is very hot, add the tuna. Cook for 2–3 minutes, depending on thickness. Turn the steaks over and continue cooking until nicely browned on the outside yet still slightly pink in the center. Remove from the heat immediately.

Meanwhile, reheat the tomatoes and olives. Divide them among the plates and top with the tuna. Scatter with the remaining basil and season with a grinding of pepper. Serve at once, with lemon wedges.

Serves 4

Preparation 10 minutes
Cooking 20 minutes

1lb (450g) medium to large, vine-ripened tomatoes
fine sea salt and freshly ground black pepper to taste
5 tbsp olive oil
2 scallions (green onions), chopped
2 garlic cloves, crushed
1 tsp fresh thyme leaves
2 tsp chopped fresh basil
6 black olives, pitted and chopped
4 tuna steaks, 5½–6oz (150–175g) each
lemon wedges to serve

"If you are at all worried about cooking fish steaks or fillets, this is a good way to do it. Preparing the tomato garnish ahead leaves you free to concentrate on cooking the fish for a few minutes. Add a little butter or oil to the pan if the fish is lean or delicate."

Farce aux épinards

Despite a reputation for preferring a cool, wet climate, spinach thrives in Provence where it is featured in many recipes. With just a little help from garlic and nutmeg, it makes a light and delicate stuffing. Although spinach stuffing is most frequently used for sardines (see p283), it is quite versatile, and particularly good in chicken, pork, and egg dishes

Rinse the spinach without drying, then put it in a non-stick sauté pan or Dutch oven and sprinkle with a pinch of coarse salt. Stir over medium–high heat until wilted. Turn into a colander and let drain for 5 minutes until cool enough to handle; then press with your hands to squeeze out excess moisture. Chop the spinach finely.

Bring the milk to a simmer in a small saucepan and remove from the heat. Melt the butter in a frying pan over medium heat. Add the spinach, then stir in the garlic and parsley. Cook for 1 minute.

Gradually stir in the hot milk. Add the nutmeg and season with salt and pepper. Simmer for 5 minutes until the liquid evaporates slightly.

Remove from the heat. Let cool before using.

Omelette aux épinards

Make Omelette aux Cébettes (p139), replacing the scallions with 4oz (115g) farce aux épinards.

Gigotines farcies aux épinards

Finely chop a slice of cured ham and mix with 8oz (225g) farce aux épinards. Spoon into 4 boned chicken thighs and secure with wooden toothpicks. Season the chicken with salt and pepper, place in a greased roasting pan, and moisten with 3 tbsp dry vermouth, such as Noilly Prat. Bake in a preheated 375°F/190°C oven for 40–45 minutes or until cooked through.

Makes about 8oz (225g)

Preparation 15 minutes
Cooking 15 minutes
1½lb (675g) young spinach leaves
coarse sea salt
¼ cup milk
fine sea salt and freshly ground
   black pepper to taste
2 tbsp unsalted butter, plus extra
   for greasing
2 garlic cloves, crushed
leaves from 3 sprigs of flat-leaf
   parsley, finely chopped
¼ tsp grated fresh nutmeg

Sardines farcies aux épinards

You know spring is in the air when sardines stuffed with spinach start appearing on the menus of Provence restaurants. When making this at home, use small sardines and take care to not overcook them. Remove the dish from the oven and check the sardines after 13-15 minutes, then return to the oven if necessary.

Preheat the oven to 400°F/200°C. Butter a *tian* or earthenware gratin dish.

To prepare the sardines, clean them under cold running water; cut off the heads with kitchen scissors, then open them up with your fingers or with a knife and remove the innards and the central spine and bones.

Open the sardines flat on the work surface, placing them skin side down with the head end nearest to you. Spread a generous teaspoon of spinach stuffing on each sardine. Roll them up, from head end to tail end.

Spread about two-thirds of the remaining spinach stuffing in the buttered baking dish. Arrange the sardines on top and cover with the rest of the spinach stuffing. Scatter with the grated Gruyère and dot with the diced butter.

Bake for 15–20 minutes until heated through. Serve hot, directly from the dish.

Serves 4

Preparation 30 minutes
Cooking 25 minutes
2 tbsp unsalted butter, diced, plus
   soft butter for greasing
12 fresh sardines, about 1¼lb
   (550g) total weight
Farce aux Epinards (p281)
¼ cup shredded Gruyère cheese
fine sea salt and freshly ground
   black pepper to taste

Clean and bone the sardines, then open them up flat, like a book, so you can spread the stuffing inside.

Maquereaux grillés aux herbes

This simple way of barbecuing or grilling mackerel with fresh herbs works best with very fresh fish. If the mackerel are very small, eat them with your fingers for a casual treat.

Serves 4

Preparation 15 minutes
Cooking 10 minutes
8 small mackerel, gutted
 and cleaned
fine sea salt and freshly ground
 black pepper to taste
¼ cup olive oil
8 sprigs of fresh thyme
8 small sprigs of flat-leaf parsley
8 small fronds of fresh dillweed
 or fennel
1 lemon, cut lengthwise into
 4 wedges

Prepare a barbecue fire or preheat the grill.

Rinse the fish well and pat dry with a clean tea towel or paper towels. Season inside with salt and pepper.

Place the fish side by side on a plate. Make a few diagonal slashes on both sides of each fish, cutting through the skin and just into the flesh. Season the outside. Drizzle with olive oil and scatter the herbs over the top.

Grill or barbecue for 3–5 minutes on each side, depending on the size of the fish. Season again. Serve at once, with lemon wedges.

Sardines grillées à l'estragon

Rinse a dozen very fresh, small sardines under cold running water and pat dry with a clean tea towel or paper towels. Season inside and out with salt and pepper, then put a sprig of fresh tarragon inside each fish. Lay the fish on a plate. Drizzle with 3 tbsp olive oil mixed with 2 tsp finely chopped fresh tarragon and turn over to coat both sides. Grill or barbecue the sardines for 2 minutes on each side—take care not to overcook. Remove at once from the heat. Rub 4 large, thick slices of toasted *pain de campagne* with the cut side of half a garlic clove, then spread with salted butter. Put the sardines on the bread, season with pepper, and eat immediately.

Cut slits in the sides of the fish and add herbs and seasonings before cooking.

dinner

Menu

tarte à la
tomate

encornets
à l'américaine

riz pilaf

meringues
aux pignons

Tarte à la tomate

This traditional tomato tart has a luscious filling with a subtle, smoky flavor. It takes some time to prepare but is not difficult, and well worth the effort. If you are short on time, use store-bought pastry and just make the filling.

Preheat the oven to 350°F/180°C. Lightly butter a 12in (30cm) tart pan with a removable bottom.

Roll out the dough thinly on a floured surface. Lift onto the pan and press in lightly without stretching. Prick with a fork. Line with parchment paper or foil and scatter in pie weights or beans. Bake for 10 minutes. Carefully remove the parchment and pie weights and bake 5 minutes longer. Take out of the oven and let cool.

Blanch and skin the tomatoes (see p90), then slice. Sprinkle them with salt and let drain in a colander.

Meanwhile, make the filling. Heat the oil in a frying pan, then add the onions and bacon. Cook over medium heat for 15 minutes, stirring frequently, until the onions are soft and golden. Add the sugar, garlic, canned tomatoes, and tomato paste. Simmer for 10 minutes or until thick, stirring occasionally. Remove the pan from the heat and let cool 10 minutes.

Turn up the oven temperature to 400°F/200°C.

In a bowl, lightly whisk the eggs to blend. Season with salt and pepper and add the oregano. Stir into the tomato mixture.

Spread the filling in the pastry shell. Arrange the drained tomato slices neatly on top. Sprinkle with the thyme and Gruyère. Bake for 30 minutes or until the eggs are cooked through. Let cool 5 minutes before serving.

Makes a 30cm (12in) tart to serve 6

Preparation 40 minutes, plus making pastry
Cooking 30 minutes

12oz (350g) savory Pâte Brisée (p213)
6–8 medium to large ripe tomatoes
2 tsp fresh thyme leaves
½ cup shredded Gruyère cheese

For the filling
1½ tbsp peanut oil
1lb (450g) mild onions, finely chopped
5 strips thick-sliced bacon, cut crosswise into ½in (1cm) strips
1 scant tsp sugar
3 garlic cloves, crushed
1 can (about 15oz diced) peeled tomatoes, drained
2 tbsp tomato paste
2 medium eggs
salt and pepper to taste
2 tsp dried oregano or marjoram

Gently cook the filling until it is thoroughly softened and reduced—it should be quite thick before you add the eggs.

Encornets à l'américaine

Squid with seafood sauce is a sumptuous dish that is perfect for entertaining. Prepare ahead, then reheat and finish just before serving.

Serves 6

Preparation 20 minutes
Cooking 1½ hours

4½lb (2kg) small to medium squid
   (calamari)
¼ cup olive oil
2 mild onions, finely chopped
fine sea salt and freshly ground
   black pepper to taste
¼ cup brandy
2 cups white wine
4 stalks dried fennel about
   4in (10cm) long, or 2 stalks
   fresh fennel
2 bay leaves
1 tbsp unsalted butter
3½oz (100g) cooked ham, diced
3 garlic cloves, crushed
5 sprigs of flat-leaf parsley,
   finely chopped
1 small hot chili, seeded and
   finely chopped
6 medium tomatoes, chopped
1 tbsp tomato paste
large pinch of saffron strands
   or powder

If the squid have not been cleaned, cut off the heads, but keep the tentacles. Pull out the innards and transparent bone. Rinse, then peel off the skin. Open up the bodies and cut into strips ½in (1cm) wide and 2½in (6cm) long. Rinse well and pat dry. Heat the oil in a large sauté pan. Add the strips of squid and the tentacles. Cover and cook over medium heat for 20 minutes, stirring occasionally. Stir in the onions and cook for another 5 minutes until soft and golden. Season with salt and pepper.

Gently warm the brandy. Drizzle it over the squid mixture and carefully ignite with a long match. Let the flames die down, then pour in the wine. Cover and cook for 15 minutes. Add 2 cups of water, the fennel, and bay leaves. Partially cover, turn up the heat a little, and let simmer for 10–15 minutes, stirring occasionally.

Meanwhile, melt the butter in a frying pan. Add the ham, then the garlic, parsley, chili, tomatoes, and tomato paste. Simmer gently, stirring, for 10 minutes.

Take the pan with the squid off the heat. Lift out the squid, fennel, and bay leaves; reserve. Put the juices from the pan in a food processor and add the ham mixture. Process until smooth. Push the mixture through a chinois or fine sieve into a bowl.

Return the squid, bay leaves, and fennel to the sauté pan. Add the sieved sauce and stir in well. Simmer over low heat for about 20 minutes, stirring from time to time and making sure the liquid doesn't reduce too quickly.

Just before serving, soften the saffron in 2 tbsp warm water. Remove and discard the fennel and bay leaves from the sauté pan. Stir the saffron water into the squid sauce and adjust the seasonings. Serve hot.

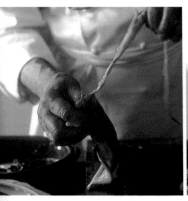

Remove the transparent bone and innards from the squid bodies, then pull or scrape off the outer skin.

Riz pilaf

A simple yet effective way to cook long-grain rice is to first sauté it in butter with a little chopped shallot and then gently simmer it in a covered pan. It will turn out fluffy and just tender, a perfect accompaniment to a seafood dish with a rich sauce such as Encornets à l'Américaine (p290). It's also good with white meat and vegetable stews.

Serves 6

Preparation 10 minutes
Cooking 25 minutes

5 tbsp unsalted butter
4 small shallots, finely chopped
1½ cups Camargue red rice or
    other long-grain rice
3–3¼ cups vegetable stock or
    water, or as needed
fine sea salt and freshly ground
    black pepper to taste

Melt half the butter in a large sauté pan. Add the shallots and cook over low heat, stirring often, for 5 minutes or until softened.

Measure the rice in a cup—you'll need twice this volume of stock or water. Reserve the rest of the liquid to add during cooking if necessary.

Add the rice to the shallots and stir for 2 minutes until the grains become coated with butter and translucent. Season with a little salt.

Add 3 cups of stock or water. Stir once, then cover the pan and cook over medium–low heat for 20 minutes, checking from time to time. Add a little more stock or water if the rice looks dry and is still tough. Continue cooking for a couple of minutes until the rice is just tender and the grains separate easily.

Cut the remaining butter into bits. Remove the rice from the heat. Fluff up the grains with a fork and adjust the seasonings. Transfer to a serving bowl and stir in the butter until melted and smooth. Serve soon.

Couscous aux raisins

The North African staple couscous—medium-grain hard wheat semolina—has found a new home in the kitchens of Provence. Try it as an alternative to rice with a seafood main course. Spiked with raisins and pleasantly fluffy, it is particularly good with squid and just simple enough to set off a rich, fragrant sauce.

Bring the stock (or a kettle of water) to a boil. Put the olive oil in a sauté pan over moderate heat. Spread in the couscous and stir to coat with oil. Check the cooking instructions on the couscous box and pour in the required amount of boiling stock or water. Season lightly with salt and pepper. Stir, then cover and reduce the heat to low (or as the package directs). Cook, stirring occasionally, for 6–8 minutes, or until the stock is absorbed.

Meanwhile, melt the butter in a small frying pan over medium heat. Add the raisins and cook, stirring frequently, for 2–3 minutes. Remove from the heat.

Take the couscous off the heat and add the buttery raisins. Stir with a fork. Cover and let stand for 5–10 minutes. Just before serving, stir again with a fork to fluff up the couscous. Adjust the seasonings.

Variation
Replace the couscous with bulgur wheat, following the same method. (Check the package instructions, as bulgur often requires more liquid and longer cooking.)

Serves 6

Preparation 5 minutes,
  plus resting
Cooking 20 minutes
2 cups vegetable stock,
  or as needed
3 tbsp olive oil
12oz (about 2 cups) pre-steamed
  or "instant" couscous
fine sea salt and freshly ground
  black pepper to taste
2 tbsp
 soft butter
3 tbsp plump raisins

"Couscous and pilaf-style rice can both be used with equal success as side dishes for fish, chicken, and lamb."

Meringues aux pignons

These meringues with pine nuts are delicious on their own, but are even better with a fruit coulis (see p136) and whisked crème fraîche. Pine nuts add an unmistakable Provence touch, although you can use toasted slivered almonds or chopped pistachio nuts instead.

Preheat the oven to 200°F/95°C, or the lowest setting.

Whisk the egg whites with 1½ tbsp of the granulated sugar and the lemon juice until the whites are soft and foamy. Add 1 tbsp of the remaining granulated sugar and continue whisking. Once the meringue mixture is firm, gradually whisk in the rest of the granulated sugar until the meringue is glossy.

Sift in the confectioners' sugar. Fold into the meringue with a large metal spoon.

Line a baking sheet with parchment paper. Using a tablespoon, shape small meringues and drop onto the parchment, spacing them about 1½in (3cm) apart. Sprinkle the meringues with the pine nuts—do not press them into the meringue.

Bake for 1¾ hours. Let cool completely in the turned-off oven.

Serve the meringues with the coulis and crème fraîche.

Serves 6

Preparation 20 minutes
Cooking 1¾ hours
3 medium egg whites
½ cup granulated sugar
½ tsp lemon juice
¾ cup confectioners' (powdered)
   sugar
¾ cup pine nuts (pignoli)

To serve
apricot coulis (p136)
chilled crème fraîche, whisked
   until thick

Space the meringues 1½in (3cm) apart on the lined baking sheet, and generously sprinkle with pine nuts without pushing them into the mixture.

sunday

In true French style, *fromages et fruits*—cheese with fruit—is the preferred Provençal way to end a meal. Discover how to make best use of the luscious local fruit. Visit an artisan goat's cheese dairy. Bid Provence *au revoir* with an accomplished farewell supper of succulent stuffed duck and *tarte à l'orange*.

La marché aux fruits

From early spring until late autumn, Provence markets display an ever-changing feast of irresistible locally grown fruits at their seasonal best. Gui picked some favorites for this morning's lesson.

Provençal melons are on sale from May until October and at their peak in the summer months. This is the best time to make the most of them—they will be deliciously fragrant and at their least expensive.

Select peaches one by one. First decide if you prefer *pêches* white (*blanches*) or yellow (*jaunes*). Make sure they aren't imported. Avoid any that are bruised, and look for a firm but not rock hard texture and a faint fragrance. Once bought, handle with care as peaches bruise easily.

Even if they look tempting on the market stall, don't buy too many sweet, plump grapes at once. Select one nice, heavy bunch, as it will always look more appetizing than two or three small bunches. Rinse the bunch under cold running water, shake gently, and let drain in a colander. Grapes are always best served at room temperature. Leftover, picked-over bunches never look good at the next meal—pick off and use the grapes in a fruit salad instead.

Fresh fruit

The growing season goes on for a very long time in the small market gardens of Provence. Look out for early ripening local fruits such as strawberries and apricots.

Although most are imported from North Africa and sometimes southern Spain, oranges and clementines always look particularly appetizing when they are carefully displayed with casual flair in Provençal market stalls. Look for fruit still attached to its stem.

When there's a glut of apricots (or other fruits such as melons, peaches, and pears), try to buy them at slightly different degrees of ripeness. Store for up to 3 days in a cool place rather than the refrigerator. Feel and smell for the perfect ones just before the meal you are planning.

Berries are very fragile and have an extremely short shelf life—it's all part of their delicate appeal. Keep them in a cool place and serve on the same day you buy them. If it's very hot, you can refrigerate raspberries, blackberries, and red and white currants, but chilling tends to destroy the fragrance of market garden strawberries such as smooth, juicy Gariguettes. Rinsing isn't absolutely necessary—do it very gently if you feel you must.

Canapés de figues au fromage de brebis

A true taste of Provence... fresh figs and creamy soft ewe's or goat's milk cheese sweetly rounded off by aromatic honey makes a great combination for a leisurely late breakfast. A quick grinding of black pepper can add a nice finishing touch.

Serves 6

Preparation 10 minutes
Cooking 15 minutes
1 fresh baguette
8 ripe figs, stemmed
8oz (225g) fresh creamy ewe's
   or goat's milk cheese
6–8 tbsp rosemary or
   lavender honey

Preheat the broiler. Cut the baguette into long, diagonal slices. Arrange them in one layer on a baking sheet and lightly toast both sides under the broiler.

Slice the figs lengthwise. Arrange on top of the toasted baguette slices. Spoon the cheese over the top, pressing it down a little.

Broil, watching carefully, for 3–4 minutes or until bubbly-hot and slightly golden at the edges.

Drizzle with the honey and serve immediately.

Cut the figs into neat slices and place on the baguette, then cover with the cheese. The topping will cook more quickly and evenly if the pieces of cheese are small.

Preparing pears

By the time a pear is perfect for eating—ripe, exuding fragrance, and yielding to the touch—it is no longer ideal for cooking. When you want to use pears to make a tart, such as the Tatin de Poires (see p306), or a cake, or to serve simply poached, choose unbruised,

Peel   Carefully peel the pears, keeping the peeling knife parallel with the skin. Use a narrow knife, straight or curved, rather than a vegetable peeler. Cut each pear in half lengthwise from core to stem end. Cut out the seeds and core.

Poach   Place the pear halves in one layer in a wide saucepan or sauté pan. Cover with simmering water or a light sugar syrup, and simmer for 2–3 minutes until just cooked. Test for tenderness with the tip of a knife. (To make a light sugar syrup, dissolve ½ cup of sugar in 2 cups water, bring to a simmer, and cook for 5 minutes before adding the pears.)

smooth specimens that feel firm but not hard and that give just a little when pressed with your finger. If you simply want to fan out a fresh pear to serve with cured ham, the best choice will be in between the two stages previously described—just ripe rather than under or fully ripe.

Drain   Lift out the pears with a slotted spoon. Drain, refresh under cold running water, and drain again; then spread on a clean tea towel or a double layer of paper towels to absorb excess moisture. Lay the pears cut-side down and cut lengthwise into thin slices, keeping the slices attached at the top.

Fan   Gently spread out the slices to make a fan shape. If you aren't using the pears immediately, sprinkle with lemon juice to prevent them from oxidizing and browning.

Tatin de poires

This caramelized pear upside-down cake is a variation on the classic apple tart of northwest France. Redolent with honey, it is typical of Provence. It can also be made with other poached fruit such as peaches, nectarines, plums, or apricots.

Serves 6-8

Preparation 50 minutes
Cooking about 50 minutes

4 ripe but firm pears, such as William's or Comice
4 tbsp rosemary or lavender honey

For the cake mixture

11 tbsp (5½oz) unsalted butter, plus extra butter for greasing
2 large eggs
⅔ cup honey
2 cups plain flour
2 tsp baking powder

Preheat the oven to 350°F/180°C. Line a 10in (24cm) moule à manqué tin or a round cake pan with parchment paper or buttered foil. Set the pan on a baking sheet.

Peel and poach the pears, then cut them into fan shapes (see pp304–305).

Put the honey in a small, heavy saucepan, bring to a boil, and let cook gently over medium heat until the honey turns a shade darker and caramelizes. Immediately pour evenly into the prepared cake pan. Arrange the pears on the caramel.

To make the cake mixture, beat the butter with a wooden spoon until very soft and creamy. Set aside. Whisk the eggs with the honey for about 10 minutes until pale and creamy. Add in the flour and baking powder, and whisk in thoroughly. Fold in the softened butter.

Carefully pour the cake mixture over the pears. Tap the pan against the work surface to remove any air bubbles and settle the mixture. Bake for 50 minutes or until the tip of a knife inserted in the center comes out clean.

Transfer to a wire rack to cool for 30 minutes. To invert, cover the cake pan with a slightly larger plate or round platter. Holding the cake pan and the plate together with both hands, turn them over so the cake is upside down on the plate. Serve slightly warm or let cool completely before serving.

Pour the bubbling honey caramel into the lined pan to create a smooth base for the pears. The caramel turns into a golden topping when you invert the cake onto a plate for serving.

Glace à la fraise

This strawberry ice cream isn't overly sweet and tastes extremely fresh and fruity. Because homemade fruit ice creams are simply prepared and contain no chemicals or preservatives, they don't remain at their best as long as commercial products. Homemade ice cream should be eaten within days rather than weeks.

Serves 6

Preparation 15 minutes,
  plus cooling and freezing
Cooking 5 minutes

4 cups ripe fresh strawberries or
  thawed frozen strawberries
½ cup sugar
1 tbsp orange juice
2 cups chilled crème fraîche

To serve

¾ cup fresh strawberries, hulled
Petits Sablés à la Lavande
  (p222), optional

If using fresh strawberries, hull them. Combine the strawberries, sugar, and orange juice in a saucepan. Bring to a boil over high heat, stirring constantly. Reduce the heat to medium and cook for 2 minutes, stirring and mashing down the strawberries. Set aside to cool a little.

Push the mixture through a fine sieve into a medium to large bowl, pressing down firmly with the back of the spoon to squeeze through as much pulp as possible. Also use the spoon to scrape off the pulp sticking to the underside of the sieve. Cover and refrigerate until needed.

In another bowl, whip the crème fraîche until firm peaks form. Fold a heaping tablespoonful into the strawberry purée to loosen it a little. Continue folding in the crème fraîche, a couple of tablespoons at a time, working lightly upward from the bottom of the bowl. Pour the mixture into an ice-cream maker and freeze according to the manufacturer's directions. When set, transfer to a suitable container and freeze until ready to serve.

Remove the ice cream from the freezer about 10 minutes before serving. Spoon into individual bowls or glasses. Serve with fresh strawberries and, if you like, lavender biscuits.

Variations

If you're not using an ice-cream maker, pour the strawberry cream into a suitable container and freeze. After about 45 minutes, remove the container from the freezer and process the ice cream mixture in a food processor for a few seconds. Return to the freezer. Repeat the process about 45 minutes later, then leave the ice cream in the freezer until completely frozen. This will have a different texture than churned ice cream, but still makes a delicious frozen dessert.

Use the same method and equal weights of fruit to prepare raspberry ice cream (using 10 tbsp sugar) and peach or apricot ice cream (using 6 tbsp sugar).

A la fromagerie

Cheeses always reflect the climate, land, and flora of the place they are made. Provence is no exception. Not being a region of lush, temperate grazing pastures and dairy culture, it traditionally produces simple cheeses that are meant to be served fresh. Local cheeses are more often made from goat's or ewe's milk than in other parts of France, where more complex cow's milk cheeses predominate.

Dairies tend to operate on a small scale and normally specialize in cheeses made from one kind of milk. Typically, an artisan dairy will produce two kinds of cheese, one smaller for quick consumption, one larger for aging.

Goats are the dairy animal most able to thrive in the dry Provençal hills dotted with sparse aromatic shrubs— ewes prefer flatter terrain and cows richer meadows. Green grass carries very little appeal for goats—they are picky eaters rather than placid grazing animals.

Despite their frisky resilience, goats are delicate creatures not fond of the rain, wind, and cold weather. Even though relatively short, winters in the high grounds of Provence can be very severe, and goats are kept indoors from November until April.

Sociable goats

Despite a reputation for being temperamental, goats are in fact fairly friendly. Occasional bouts of head butting establish who is boss but it's not a real problem as long as there is plenty of space for the goats to feed, with easy access to water troughs so no dominant animal can keep the others away.

Milking

Just like very small dairy cows, goats are milked twice a day, first early in the morning and again late in the afternoon. They seem to enjoy the whole process, cleverly anticipating just where they have to go.
▽

△
The herds

Goats produce milk during at least 5 years, with 1½–2 months off every year just before and after they give birth, usually to twin kids. Only the female kids are kept—the only two or three males in the herd are the rams.

Goat's milk Fresh goat's milk has a lovely clean taste, with very subtle hints of lemon and straw. Its fat globules are smaller than those found in cow's milk, which makes it—and the cheese produced from it—easier to digest.

▽

△

Making cheese In the very early stages of the cheesemaking process, within hours of milking, the coagulated milk starts to look thick and creamy. The curd and the whey—the solids and the liquid—gradually become distinct and separate. It takes nearly 3 quarts of goat's milk to produce a 4oz (110g) cheese.

"Goats are very sensitive creatures, a bit like children when you get to know them. They also like a bit of a fuss—and they hate being rushed, especially at milking time."

The three "ages" of goat's cheese

Fresh farmhouse goat's milk cheeses gradually develop a natural rind as they dry. Provided they are handled with care by the cheesemaker or retailer, they can be sold at different degrees of ripeness to suit the tastes of customers.

△

Youth The cheese is very soft, a little loose-textured, almost wet. It has a mild taste and its distinctive goat flavor is still very hard to detect. Creamy white and practically rindless, after about 10–14 days it begins to acquire a little fuzzy white surface mold.

△

Maturity The cheese has tightened up and lost some moisture, and is starting to develop a thin rind with small patches of blue mold. Its texture is becoming firmer and denser, and its aroma and flavor are by now unmistakably goat-like.

△

Ripe old age The cheese has shrunk, the rind has become thicker, almost wrinkly, and the blue mold has spread. The inside is very firm, sometimes almost splintery, and the taste is pleasingly pungent and a little nutty.

"Don't let a moldy or crusty rind put you off... it helps with the ripening process and can easily be scraped or cut off before you enjoy the lovely mature cheese inside."

Traditional tomme

The matured cheese of the mountains of Provence is *tomme*, which is aged for at least 3 months and can be kept for up to 10 months. Tomme has a much drier, more full-bodied and complex texture than fresh, soft cheeses.

Packed with flavor Tomme comes in different sizes. It can be log-shaped, but is usually thick, round, and flat, with a furry, blotchy (not meant to be eaten) rind protecting the dense, nutty, slightly springy-textured cheese.

△

Rich milk Tomme is usually made from cow's milk, or from ewe's or goat's milk. 2 gallons of milk go into each kilo (2¼lb) of finished tomme, making it a very nutritious food.

Pêches au jambon cru et au fenouil

Cured ham, peeled peaches, and wedges of fennel take minutes to assemble and make a lovely salty-sweet combination. Along with some good bread, this easy dish is a perfect quick lunch in summer.

Serves 4

Preparation 15 minutes,
Cooking 2 minutes
4 ripe peaches
1 small fennel bulb
12 thin slices cured ham
extra virgin olive oil for drizzling
freshly ground black pepper
  to taste

Immerse the peaches in a saucepan of boiling water for about 1 minute. Lift out of the water with a slotted spoon and check to see if the skin will slip off easily. If it does not, boil 1 minute longer. Refresh under cold running water and drain again, then peel off the skins. Halve the peaches and remove the pits. Cut each half lengthwise into 2 wedges.

Quarter the fennel bulb lengthwise. Cut out the core, then cut each quarter lengthwise into 2 or 3 slices.

Arrange the peach quarters, fennel slices, and cured ham on a platter. Drizzle with extra virgin olive oil and add a generous sprinkling of freshly ground pepper.

Variations
You can replace the peaches with nectarines, wedges of ripe melon, or slices of ripe pear. Just rinse the nectarines; there is no need to peel. Let your guests peel their own pears, if they wish. All these fruits make good partners for both the cured ham and the fennel.

"Remember that Roquefort and mature Gruyère are also good matches for fruit and fennel when a meat-free combination is required."

Plateau de fromage

Selecting cheeses for a cheeseboard is an enjoyable skill to acquire. Take into account the other courses you are planning to serve, your budget (good cheeses never come cheap), and the specialties of the region. While in Provence, it's more fun and more sensible to make the most of the local cheeses. Of course you would be able to buy a ripe Camembert in a good cheese shop, but take the opportunity instead to try Provençal artisan cheeses. Unlike Camembert, Brie, and Roquefort, they are not often produced on a large enough scale to be sold outside their region of origin. The cheeses shown here are (left to right): a very ripe, plain goat's milk cheese; a ewe's milk cheese topped with ash; an artisan cheese made from a mixture of ewe's and goat's milk; and a tomme de brebis.

A good idea is to go for a mixture of goat's and ewe's milk cheeses. A fresh goat's cheese left to mature until slightly denser and coated with a dusting of ash will contrast well with a distinctly pungent but creamy soft, matured ewe's milk cheese. Many Provence cheeses are flavored and presented with herbs and leaves, and some are made with a delicately balanced mixture of goat's and ewe's milk. Ewe's milk tomme is mild and aromatic, with a nutty creamy texture. It's likely to please a majority of guests.

How many different cheeses? There's no real rule, but the tradition is to serve either a single cheese or at least three.

When serving the goat's cheeses typical of Provence, if they are young drizzle them with honey and serve with fresh figs, peaches, or apricots; serve mature goat's cheeses with grapes or cherries or a chunk of fresh bread. Enjoy ripe goat's cheeses on their own, perhaps with a glass of rosé or white wine.

Pêches au vin rosé

Peaches poached in rosé wine with a touch of orange flower water make a light, grown-up dessert. Nectarines and pears are also very good prepared this way. Pears will need to be poached for 5-6 minutes before peeling; nectarines can be left unpeeled.

Serves 4

Preparation and cooking
  15 minutes, plus chilling
4 white peaches
3 tbsp sugar
1 tbsp orange flower water
about 2 cups rosé wine, chilled
a few fresh basil or mint leaves
  for garnish

Immerse the peaches in a saucepan of boiling water for 1–2 minutes. Lift out of the water with a slotted spoon and check to see if the skin will slip off easily. If not, boil 1 minute longer. Refresh under cold running water and drain again, then peel off the skins.

Cut the peaches in half and take out the pits. Reshape the peaches and place one in each of 4 wine glasses or bowls. Sprinkle the peaches with the sugar and orange flower water.

Pour in chilled rosé to cover the peaches completely. Refrigerate for at least 1 hour or until ready to serve.

Arrange a leaf or two of basil or mint on top of each peach before serving.

Pêches au sirop d'orange

You can make a non-alcoholic version of this dessert by replacing the rosé wine with a light orange syrup. Combine 6 tbsp sugar, 2 cups water, 2 tbsp orange flower water, and 1 tbsp each finely grated orange and lemon zest in a saucepan. Bring to a simmer and cook for 5 minutes. Let cool, then strain through a sieve and discard the zest. Chill the syrup before pouring it over the peeled peaches.

Gelée de coings

This deliciously tart quince jelly is particularly good with pork and worthwhile trying with cheese, such as tomme de brebis and other aged ewe's milk cheeses.

Peel and slice the quinces. Put them in a sauté pan with the peppercorns and bay leaves. Cover with boiling water, bring to a simmer, and cook for about 45 minutes or until the quinces are very soft. Remove from the heat and let cool a little, then drain.

Briefly dip a piece of unbleached muslin cloth in boiling water. When it is cool enough to handle, squeeze out the excess water. Lay it flat and put the quinces in the middle. Lift up and secure the sides of the muslin to make a bag. Suspend the muslin bag over a bowl and let the quince juice drip through for at least 12 hours.

Discard the pulp and flavorings left in the bag. Measure the juice. For each 1 cup juice, you need ¾ cup sugar and 1½ tsp orange juice.

Put the quince juice, sugar, and orange juice in a saucepan and bring to a simmer over low heat, stirring until the sugar has dissolved. Turn up the heat a little, bring to a boil, and cook without stirring for 10 minutes. Skim off and discard any foam from the surface. Remove from the heat and let the jelly cool a little.

Meanwhile, immerse 2 small jam jars about 1 cup (8oz) each in boiling water; remove and let dry.

Spoon the jelly into the sterilized jars, cover, and let cool to room temperature. Refrigerate and use within 2 months.

Variation
Another idea for quinces is to poach them whole in a light sugar syrup (see p322) for 50–60 minutes or until just tender. Drain, refresh under cold running water, and drain again, then peel. They can then be frozen for up to 3 months.

Makes about 2 (8oz) jars of jelly

Preparation 30 minutes, plus straining
Cooking 1 hour
1½–1¾lb (675–750g) quinces
5 black peppercorns
3 bay leaves
sugar
orange juice

"Make the most of quinces while they are available. Their season in late autumn is all too short."

Salade aux fruits cuits

This lovely fruit compote is very good on its own, or served with plain creamy yogurt or basil ice cream (p244).

To peel the peaches and pears, immerse them in a saucepan of boiling water and cook the peaches for 1–2 minutes and the pears for 3–4 minutes. Lift the fruits out of the water with a slotted spoon, refresh under cold running water, and drain again; then peel off the skins. Cut the peaches and pears in half and remove the pits or cores. Cut the fruit into quarters.

Cut the lemon into 8 slices and remove any seeds. Put the slices in a sauté pan with the sugar and 3½ cups water. Bring to a simmer and cook for 5 minutes over medium heat. Meanwhile, halve the plums and apricots and remove the pits.

Add the peaches to the simmering syrup. Return to a simmer, then add the pears. Bring back to a simmer, then add the apricots. When the syrup is simmering again, gently drop in the plums. Let simmer for 5 minutes.

Remove from the heat and let cool for a few minutes. Lift out the fruit with a slotted spoon and place in a shallow serving bowl. Set aside to cool.

Meanwhile, boil the pan of syrup over high heat until thickened and reduced by one-third. Let cool, then discard the lemon slices and spoon the syrup over the fruit. Refrigerate until ready to eat. Garnish with mint or basil sprigs before serving.

Serves 6

Preparation 15 minutes,
  plus cooling
Cooking 30 minutes
4 peaches
3 pears
1 lemon
1 cup sugar
6 plums
6 apricots
a few small fresh mint or basil
  sprigs for garnish

Cut lemon slices to flavor the poaching syrup. Use an unwaxed lemon, or scrub the fruit with warm soapy water and rinse well.

Oreillettes

These little fried pastry "ears" are best eaten immediately. They are the perfect sweet snack to enjoy with a cup of coffee or hot chocolate.

Makes 10-12 pastries

Preparation 30 minutes,
  plus resting
Cooking 15 minutes

1 stick (4oz) unsalted butter
4 cups plain flour, plus extra for
  dredging
1 tsp baking powder
grated zest of 1 lemon
grated zest of 2 oranges
juice of 1 orange
4 medium egg yolks
2 heaping tbsp granulated sugar
½ tsp salt
3 tbsp milk
1 tbsp rum
about 4 cups peanut oil for frying
confectioners' (powdered) sugar
  for dusting

Melt the butter gently in a small saucepan. Mix together the flour, baking powder, and grated lemon and orange zests in a large bowl.

Make a well in the center and put in the orange juice, egg yolks, melted butter, granulated sugar, salt, milk, and rum. Blend the ingredients in the well with your fingertips, then mix in the flour and knead firmly into a smooth dough.

Gather the dough into a ball. Dust with flour and wrap in a clean tea towel. Enclose loosely in a plastic bag and refrigerate for 4–6 hours or overnight.

Dredge a work surface with flour and roll out the dough very thinly (about the thickness of a nickel). Using a pastry cutter, make 1¼ x 6in (3 x 15cm) rectangles. Cut each rectangle into 2 or 3 small triangles. Use the tip of a sharp knife to slit each triangle in the middle, then tuck the pointed top of the triangle into the slit.

Bring about 2in (5cm) oil—enough oil to completely cover the pastries—to a simmer in a deep sauté pan over medium–high heat. As soon as the oil bubbles, carefully fry the pastries for 1–2 minutes until golden all over. Stir with long tongs after a minute to check they are coloring evenly; turn them over if they aren't.

Lift out the pastries with a slotted spoon and drain well on a double layer of paper towels. Let sit just until cool enough to handle, then dust with sifted confectioners' sugar and serve.

Cut small triangles from the rolled dough, then quickly fold each into a little ear shape.

Drying orange peel

Strips of orange peel dried over the hearth (or, less poetically, in a warm place such as a cupboard) are a favorite Provençal ingredient. They play an essential role in flavoring daubes and fish stews, among other things. Whenever you are using the zest or

Cut   Hold an orange firmly in one hand. Use whichever small, sharp knife you feel comfortable with—a vegetable peeler or a straight or curved paring knife. Holding the blade of the knife almost parallel to the orange, start cutting a strip of peel near the stem end.

Peel   Try not to cut into the flesh of the orange—leave it protected by a thin layer of white pith. Work in circles, gently easing the knife around between the pith and the peel, at the same time gradually turning the orange with your other hand.

peel of oranges (or other citrus fruit), try to buy unwaxed or organic fruit, because standard oranges tend to have a waxy coating of chemical preservatives. If in doubt, first gently scrub oranges in warm soapy water, then rinse thoroughly, drain, and pat dry.

Keep peeling   Longer strips will dry better than shorter pieces, so try to lift off as long a ribbon of peel as you can.

Dry   Put the ribbons of orange peel in a dry, warm place—suspended from a hook where you hang utensils near the oven is a good spot. The strips will be dry enough in 2 or 3 days, and you can keep them for up to 3 weeks, stored in an airtight container or a screwtop jar. Or store them in a jar of confectioners' sugar—they will lend a delicious flavor to the sugar.

Confiture d'oranges

This orange marmalade is easy to make, looks bright, and tastes fresh and zesty. Try to make it using unwaxed or organic oranges, if possible. You can replace one or two oranges with a lemon and/or grapefruit if you like. Simply check that the total weight of fruit remains the same.

Makes 4 (8oz) jars

Preparation 15 minutes,
  plus cooling overnight
Cooking 2½ hours
2¼lb (1kg) oranges
2¼lb (about 5 cups) sugar
juice of 1 orange (about ⅓ cup)

Scrub the oranges well with warm soapy water, then rinse. Put them in a saucepan and add 4 cups water. Bring to a boil, then cover and cook over medium heat for 2 hours. (Adjust the heat, if needed, to be sure the water does not evaporate completely.) Remove from the heat and let the oranges cool overnight in the covered pan.

Lift out the oranges with a slotted spoon. Cut them in half and scoop out the flesh and pith. Reserve the peel. Return the flesh and pith to the liquid in the saucepan.

Bring to a boil and cook vigorously for about 5 minutes to reduce the liquid to about 3 cups. Strain the liquid into a heatproof pitcher or bowl. Discard the flesh, pith, and any seeds.

Rinse out the saucepan. Slice the orange peel into thin strips. Return the liquid and peel to the pan. Add the sugar and orange juice.

Bring to a boil over a high heat, stirring until the sugar has dissolved. Stop stirring and let bubble for about 20 minutes. Test by putting a teaspoon of marmalade on a saucer and freeze for 1 minute. Take it out of the freezer and press gently with your index finger—it should yield to the pressure but "bounce" back. If it is still runny, cook for 2–3 more minutes and repeat the test.

While the marmalade is cooking, sterilize 4 small jam jars (about 1 cup/8oz each). Immerse them in boiling water, remove, and let dry.

Spoon the marmalade into the sterilized jars, cover, and let cool to room temperature. Refrigerate up to 4 months.

Écorces d'orange confites

Caramelized orange strips are a versatile ingredient, equally at home in sweet and savory dishes. Try adding to roast duck, at the same time using the juice of the orange to deglaze the roasting pan. They are also good with pot-roasted pork tenderloin and with beef casseroles.

Put the sugar in a saucepan with ¾ cup of water. Stir over medium heat until the sugar has dissolved, then let cook gently for 3 minutes.

Meanwhile, cut away the colored zest from the orange, leaving the bitter white pith behind. Then cut the zest into matchstick-size pieces. Add to the syrup and simmer gently for 15 minutes. Lift out with a spoon and drain well in a sieve.

Pack between layers of parchment paper in an airtight box and use within 3 days. Alternatively, freeze for up to 1 month.

Serves 4-6 as a garnish
  or flavoring

Preparation and cooking
  30 minutes
5 tbsp sugar
1 large orange

Salade d'oranges

Marinated orange salad is the lightest and freshest of winter desserts and is perfect for rounding off a very hearty meal. Serve with Madeleines (p225), Oreillettes (p326), or the little pine nut cookies on p220.

Peel the oranges, removing all the white pith. Cut the oranges into thin slices. Put in a shallow bowl, sprinkle with the brandy, and let sit to macerate in a cool place for about 1 hour.

To make the syrup, put the sugar in a saucepan with 1¾ cups water and the orange zest. Cook over medium heat, stirring until the sugar has dissolved, then let bubble for 10 minutes without stirring.

Remove from the heat and stir in the orange flower water. Let sit until cool, then cover and refrigerate.

Spoon the cold syrup over the marinated oranges and stir gently. Serve chilled.

Serves 4-5

Preparation 20 minutes,
  plus macerating
Cooking 20 minutes
4 oranges
4 tbsp brandy
For the syrup
6 heaping tbsp sugar
1 tbsp finely grated orange zest
2 tbsp orange flower water

dinner

Menu

pommes d'amour
au chèvre chaud

canard farci
à la mode de
Provence

tarte à l'orange

Pommes d'amour au chèvre chaud

Tomatoes with savory and hot goat's cheese make an elegant starter or a light main course. They can be served with a small salad as suggested below; or, for a simpler alternative, serve with fresh basil leaves, black olives, or radishes.

Cut a "lid" from the stalk end of each tomato. If necessary, trim the base to enable the tomato to stand upright. Using a teaspoon, cut out the flesh and pulp without breaking the skin. Reserve the flesh; discard the seeds and white parts. Season the insides of the tomatoes with a little salt. Turn upside down in a colander to drain.

Meanwhile, combine the lemon juice with 3 tbsp water in a saucepan. Bring to a boil. Season with salt and pepper and whisk in half of the butter, then return to a boil, still whisking. Add the bunch of savory to the boiling mixture. Remove from the heat, cover, and let sit for 10–15 minutes to blend and infuse flavors.

Cut the remaining stick of butter into ½in dice and place in the bowl of a food processor. Strain the infusion into the bowl, discarding the savory sprigs. Process for 1 minute. Spoon the savory butter into the top of a double broiler (or a heatproof bowl set over a pan of boiling water). Keep hot.

Preheat the oven to 425°F/220°C.

Using a fork, gently mash half the goat cheese. Season with a little pepper and spoon into the tomatoes. Cut the remaining cheese into 6 slices and place one on top of each tomato. Put the tomatoes on a non-stick baking sheet. Bake in the upper third of the oven for 5–6 minutes or until bubbly-hot and golden at the edges.

Set a tomato on each plate and replace the lids if you like. Spoon the savory infusion around the tomato. Garnish with lightly dressed mesclun and serve soon.

Serves 6

Preparation 20 minutes
Cooking 35 minutes
6 vine-ripened medium tomatoes
fine sea salt and freshly ground
    black pepper to taste
juice of 1 lemon
2 sticks (8oz) unsalted butter
small bunch of fresh summer
    savory or thyme
1 log (about 11oz) fresh goat's
    cheese
To serve
Mesclun Citronnette (p89)

Infuse the buttery juice mixture with summer savory. Keep the infusion hot over a pan of simmering water until ready to spoon around the tomatoes.

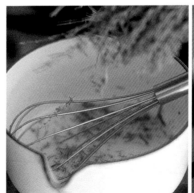

Farce aux figues et aux anchois

Sweet and salty at the same time, this fig, anchovy, and juniper stuffing is rich with fruit flavor. It can be used with many different meats, game birds, and poultry. Try it with boned shoulder or leg of lamb, or use it to stuff pork chops or a boned rolled pork roast. Its fruitiness also suits roast duck perfectly (see the recipe on p338) and it is rich and moist enough to balance the mild gaminess of pheasant, partridge, and wild rabbit.

Makes enough to stuff
1 large duck

Preparation and cooking
about 1 hour
8 plump dried figs
5 anchovy fillets
5 tbsp olive oil
2 leeks, trimmed and chopped
5 juniper berries, washed
1 tbsp fresh thyme leaves
fine sea salt and freshly ground
black pepper to taste
1 medium egg

Chop the figs. If using anchovy fillets packed in oil, drain them; rinse salted anchovies. Chop the anchovies.

Heat 3 tbsp of the olive oil in a large sauté pan. Add the figs and sauté briefly, stirring occasionally, over medium heat until softened. Remove from the pan with a slotted spoon and place in a bowl. Let cool.

Heat the rest of the oil in the pan. Add the leeks and cook, stirring, for 1 minute. Moisten with 2 tbsp water and continue cooking for 5 minutes or until softened. Add the anchovies, juniper berries, and thyme. Cook for 10–15 minutes, stirring frequently. Let cool for 5–10 minutes.

Add the anchovy mixture to the figs in the bowl. Season lightly with salt (remember the anchovies are salty) and more generously with pepper, then stir in the egg. (If you aren't planning to use the stuffing immediately, omit the egg at this point; cover with plastic wrap, and chill for up to 24 hours. Alternatively, freeze for up to 1 month. Just before using, thaw if needed, and mix in the egg).

Variations

Instead of dried figs, the stuffing can be made with 6 just-ripe but firm, fresh figs. Remove the stems before chopping them.

When using this stuffing for poultry, if the fresh liver is available, rinse it well, pat dry with paper towels, and trim, removing any whitish membrane. Chop it finely and add to the mixture to cook at the same time as the anchovies.

Canard farci à la mode de Provence

Sweet and salty fruit combinations are a traditional Mediterranean way of stuffing birds and roasted meats for festive occasions. This duck with a fig and anchovy stuffing is particularly good served alongside carrots with green olives (p76).

Serves 6

Preparation 10 minutes,
  plus chilling 30 minutes
Roasting about 1¾ hours
Farce aux Figues et aux Anchois
  (p336)
1 large duck, with liver if available
fine sea salt and freshly ground
  black pepper to taste

Using a tablespoon, put the fig stuffing into the cavity of the duck, making sure you don't pack it in too tightly. Secure the opening with crumbled piece of parchment paper. Season the duck, rubbing the salt and pepper into the skin. Cover and refrigerate for at least 30 minutes.

Preheat the oven to 425°F/220°C.

Place the duck in a roasting pan and pour in 1¼ cups of water. Cover loosely with foil. Roast for 50 minutes, then reduce the oven temperature to 350°F/180°C. Take the duck out of the oven and remove the foil. Return to the oven to roast for another 30 minutes or until the duck is cooked through. To test, push a skewer through the thickest part of the leg near the breast and check that the juices run clear. If not, continue roasting for 10 minutes or so, then test again.

Remove the duck from the oven. Cover loosely with foil and let sit in a warm place to rest for 5–10 minutes. Remove the parchment paper before serving.

Use a crumbled-up piece of parchment paper to keep the stuffing inside the duck.

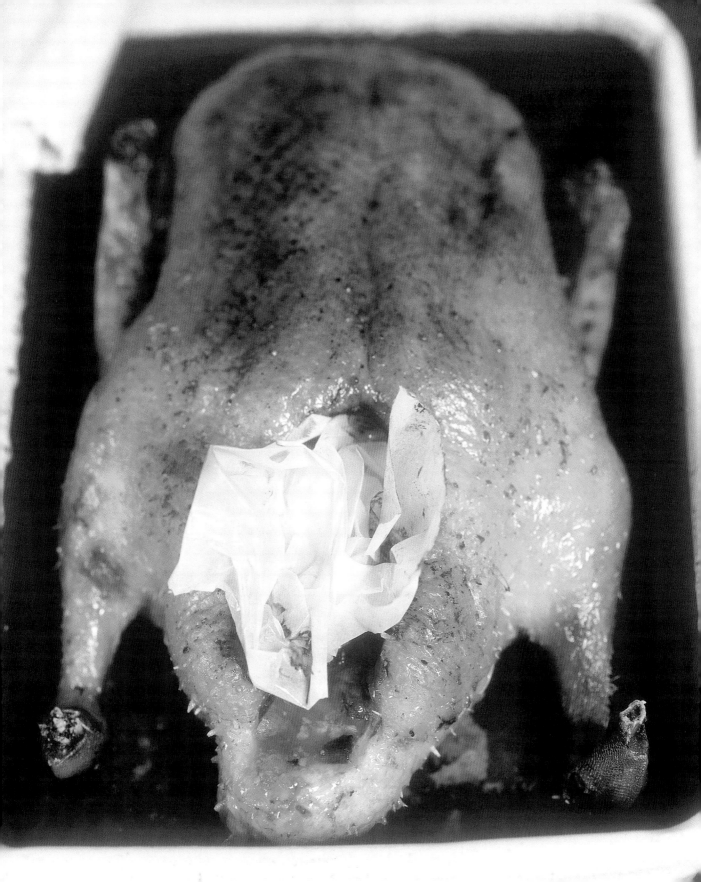

Tarte à l'orange

Deliciously pretty little orange tarts are a great way to end a special meal. You can use the same method to make lemon tarts—simply replace the oranges with 2 large, unwaxed lemons.

Makes 6 (3-4in) tartlets

Preparation 30 minutes,
  plus making pastry
Cooking 30 minutes
14oz (400g) Pâte Brisée (p213)
soft butter for greasing the pans

For the filling
grated zest and juice of 2 oranges
2 medium eggs
2 medium egg yolks
1 cup heavy (whipping) cream
1 cup sugar

For the orange topping
1 small orange
5 tbsp caster sugar

Preheat the oven to 350°F/180°C. Grease 6 tartlet tins with removeable bottoms.

Roll out the pastry dough thinly on a floured work surface. Lift onto the tins and press into them lightly with your hands without stretching the pastry. Prick each pastry case with a fork. Bake for 10 minutes. Take the pastry cases out of the oven and let cool. Trim off excess pastry. Reserve the cases.

Turn up the oven up to 400°F/200°C. To make the filling, combine the orange zest and juice, eggs, and yolks in a bowl. Whisk until slightly frothy. Add the cream and sugar, and whisk vigorously to mix. Spoon the filling into the pastry cases. Bake for 18–20 minutes or until just set.

Meanwhile, prepare the orange topping. Thinly slice the orange. Put the sugar in a saucepan with 1 cup of water. Stir over medium heat until the sugar has dissolved, then cook without stirring for 3 minutes. Add the orange slices and simmer gently for 15 minutes. Lift out the slices with tongs and drain on a rack placed over a plate. Garnish the top of each tart with a caramelized orange slice. Serve soon.

Variation

To make a large tart to serve 6, use a 12in (30cm) pan with a removeable bottom. Gently press the pastry into the tin, then prick with a fork, line with parchment paper, and fill with pie weights or dried beans. Bake for 15 minutes. Let cool. Remove the parchment and beans. Once filled, bake for 30–40 minutes or until just set. To finish, garnish the top with the caramelized orange slices.

Use a citrus reamer to squeeze all the juice from the orange, discarding any seeds. Whisk in the eggs and yolks until just blended and slightly frothy.

Glossary

agneau lamb

ail garlic; *gousse d'ail* is a garlic clove

aïoli garlicky sauce of eggs and olive oil with a mayonnaise texture; *aïoli complet* or *aïoli garni* is a dish of vegetables and salt cod served with aïoli; also known as *ailloli* and *beurre de Provence*

allumettes literally "matchsticks"; puff pastry strips; also deep-fried matchstick potatoes

amuse-bouche literally "mouth amuser"; a small appetizer, often served with apéritifs

anchois anchovy

anchoïade savory paste of anchovies, olive oil, and garlic

ancienne (à l') in the style of the "old school" or traditional

anis anise seed; also an anise-flavored apéritif (also see pastis)

apéritif alcoholic drink taken before a meal

aromates seasoning, e.g. spices and herbs

artichaut artichoke

asperge(s) asparagus; *pointe d'asperges* is an asparagus tip

baguette long, thin loaf of white bread with a crisp crust

barigoule wild mushroom similar to *mousseron*; a dish named *à la barigoule* includes ham and mushrooms

basilic basil

bâton literally "stick," this is a loaf of white bread, smaller than a baguette

batterie de cuisine tools and pans used in a kitchen

baudroie monkfish (also called *lotte*)

beignet fritter, sweet or savory

beurre butter; *beurre doux* is unsalted, while *beurre demi-sel* is slightly salted

beurre composé literally "mixed butter," this is butter flavored with herbs, anchovies, lemon zest, or other aromatics

beurre noisette butter melted and cooked until it is the color of hazelnut shells

boeuf beef

boulangère (à la) literally "baker's style," this denotes a dish that is usually cooked in the oven, often on a bed of potatoes

boulangerie bakery, baker's shop

bouquet garni a bundle of herbs and sometimes vegetables, usually tied together with string, used to flavor soups and stews; a bouquet garni is removed before serving

brandade warm garlicky purée of salt cod, cream, and sometimes mashed potatoes

brebis sheep/ewe

brouillé scrambled

brouillade scrambled eggs

brugnon nectarine

cabillaud fresh cod

caille quail

canapé small, usually decorative cocktail snack, often eaten in one bite; traditionally it has a crisp bread base

canard duck; *caneton* is a duckling

cardon cardoon, a large, celery-like vegetable in the artichoke family

cébette scallion (green onion)

céleri celery

céleri-rave celeriac (celery root)

cèpe cèpe or porcini mushroom

champignon mushroom

charcuterie assorted cold meats (often pork) and sausages/salamis; also a shop selling prepared and cooked pork, pâtés, etc.

chaud(e) hot or warm

chèvre goat; cheese made from goat's milk

chocolat chocolate; *chocolat au lait* is milk chocolate and *chocolat à croquer* is dark chocolate;

someone who makes chocolates is a *chocolatier*

citron lemon

clovisse variety of tiny clam

coing quince

confit(es) preserve or conserve, which can be either sweet or savory (fruit or vegetables preserved in sugar, alcohol, or vinegar; pieces of duck, goose, or pork cooked and preserved in their own fat)

confiture jam or fruit preserve

corail coral-colored egg sac found in scallops, sea urchins, and other seafood

coriandre coriander (cilantro)

côtes ribs or chops; cotelettes are smaller chops

coulis liquid purée, usually fruit

crème cream; *crème fleurette* is a light cream similar to whipping cream, *crème fraîche* is slightly soured cream, and *crème fouettée* is whipped cream; *crème* is also used for custard sauce and other creamy sauces and desserts

croûton small piece or slice of fried or baked bread

crudités raw vegetables

cuit(e) cooked; *bien cuit(e)*, or well cooked, is applied to steak (well done) and bread (high baked)

daube stew of meat, usually beef, braised in red wine

daubière the traditional deep, glazed earthenware cooking pot used for a daube

daurade Mediterranean variety of golden sea bream (porgy)

dégorger to remove bitterness or impurities from food before cooking, by soaking or sprinkling with salt and draining

demie (une) half a baguette

échalote shallot

écorce peel from fruit, in particular oranges; also cinnamon bark

écumoire flat perforated spoon or spatula used for skimming foam from cooking liquids and for lifting ingredients out of cooking pots

encornet small squid (also called *calamar/calmar*)

épinards spinach

estouffade Provençal term for a slow-simmered stew of meat cooked in a sealed pot with wine, herbs, and vegetables; from the verb *estoufa*, literally "to smother"; the dish can also be described as *à l'estoufado*

estragon tarragon

étouffée cooked in a sealed pot with little or no liquid (see *estouffade*)

farci(es) stuffed; the stuffing is called a *farce*

fenouil fennel, both the vegetable and herb; *graines de fenouil* are fennel seeds, used as a spice

feuilleté(e) made with puff pastry (*pâte feuilletée*)

fève fava bean

figue fig

fond base or bottom; *fond d'artichaut* is the meaty artichoke base; for smaller or baby artichokes, where there is no choke, the base is called the heart, or *coeur*

fondue melted; used for vegetables cooked long and slow until melted to a pulp; also a communal dish, often of melted cheese, served in an earthenware pot set over a small burner

fraîche/frais fresh or cool

fraise strawberry; wild strawberries are *fraises des bois*

framboise raspberry; also the name of a raspberry spirit or eau-de-vie

fromage cheese

fromagerie dairy, cheese shop

fumé(e) smoked or cured

fumet fish stock; also aroma or bouquet of wine

gâteau(x) cake(s), sweet or savory

gelée jelly

gigot leg of mutton or lamb

(*gigot d'agneau*)

gigotine part-boned and stuffed chicken leg

glace ice cream

gratin preparation browned under the broiler or in the oven, often with a topping of bread crumbs or grated cheese

gressins Provençal term for breadsticks (Italian *grissini*)

grillé(e) grilled or toasted

haricot vert green bean, usually thin "French" bean

herbe herb

huile oil; olive oil is *huile d'olive*; peanut oil is *huile d'arachides*; walnut oil is *huile de noix*

infusion liquid flavored ("infused") with herbs and other aromatics; also herbal tea or tisane

jambon ham, usually cooked (*cuit*); *jambon cru* is salt-cured ham that has been aged and air-dried rather than cooked, to be eaten raw; *jambon fumé* is smoked ham

langoustine crustacean that looks like a small lobster; in English also called Dublin Bay prawn

lapin rabbit

lardons cubes or dice of bacon

lavande lavender

loup de mer sea bass (also *bar*)

maison (de la) literally "of the house"; homemade, or the

specialty of a restaurant

maquereau mackerel

marché market

marinade mixture of wine and aromatic flavorings in which food is immersed to season, moisturize, or tenderize it before cooking

marinière (à la) literally "boatman's style"

marjolaine marjoram

mesclun from the Provençal *mescia*—"to mix": assorted small, young salad leaves

mezzaluna two-handled knife with a wide, curved blade; used by rocking the blade side to side

miel honey

miette crumb or shred/flake

morue salt cod; confusingly, *morue fraîche* is used for fresh cod (*cabillaud*)

moule mussel

mouli-légumes vegetable or food mill

mousse literally "froth" or "foam"; light, airy mixture that may be sweet or savory

mousseline light, delicate sauce or dish, often containing whipped cream or whisked egg whites

noisette hazelnut; applied to sauces and preparations that are nut-shaped or nut-colored; also a small round lamb or veal steak

nouilles noodles

noix nut; walnut

oeuf egg

oursin sea urchin

pain bread or loaf; *pain de campagne* is rustic country-style bread; *pain complet* or *entier* is wholewheat bread; *pain au levain* is sourdough bread

palet literally "disk"

papeton mousse, or flan (the principle ingredient is usually eggplant or zucchini); also fried and puréed eggplant cooked in a ring mold

pastis anise-flavored apéritif

pâte pastry, dough, or batter

pâte brisée shortcrust pastry

pâtisserie pastries and cakes; also cake or pastry shop

pâtissier, pâtissière pastry cook

pêche peach

persil parsley; *persil frisé* is curly parsley and *persil plat* is flat-leaf parsley; *persillé(e)* means parsleyed or sprinkled with chopped parsley

persillade finely chopped mixture of garlic and parsley

petit(e) small or little

pignons pine nuts

pilaf rice cooked with stock

pintade guinea fowl

pistou pounded sauce of basil, garlic, and olive oil; this is the Provençal equivalent of Italian pesto, without the pine nuts

plateau large platter or tray

poêle (à la) pan-fried

poire pear

pois chiches chickpeas (garbanzo beans)

poisson fish

poivre pepper; *poivre gris* or *noir* is black pepper and *poivre en grains* are peppercorns

poivron sweet pepper

pommade thick purée or cream

pomme apple

pomme d'amour literally "apple of love", a term affectionately used for tomato

pomme de terre potato

porc pork

poulet chicken (other words for chicken are *poularde*, *chapon*, and *coq*); *poulet fermier* is a free-range chicken, of which poulet de Bresse, fed on maize and buckwheat, is the most famous

poutargue/boutargue salty paste prepared from dried, salted, and pressed mullet or tuna roe, mashed with oil

poutine small baby anchovies

praire type of small clam

riz rice

romarin rosemary

rôti(es) roast

rouget red mullet

roustide local savory on a slice of fresh baguette; often sold in market stalls

sablé literally "sandy," this is a shortbread-like cookie; *pâte sablée* is a sweet, crumbly pastry

safran saffron

salade salad

sarriette summer savory; in Provence also called *poivre d'âne*

saucisse fresh, smoked, or dried sausage that needs to be cooked before eating

saucisson cooked or dried (*saucisson sec*) sausage that is sliced and eaten cold, usually as a first course

sauge sage

saveur(s) flavor(s)

sec, sèche dry or dried

sirop syrup

soupe soup that is usually based on vegetables (another word for soup is *potage*)

tapenade thick paste of capers, black olives, and olive oil, and sometimes anchovies; best known as an hors d'oeuvre spread on

toast but has many other uses

tapeno Provençal word for capers

tatin from Tarte Tatin, a caramelized upside-down apple tart; word is now more widely used for other upside-down tarts, both sweet and savory

thon tuna

tian shallow earthenware dish that can be rectangular, oval, or round; preparations cooked in the dish may be called tians

tomate tomato; *coeur de boeuf* is a local name for beef tomatoes

truffe truffle, an expensive and highly prized fungus with a very strong, pungent flavor; winter truffle markets can be found in towns and villages across Provence between November and March

vanille vanilla

veau veal

vert(e) green

viande meat

vin (blanc, rouge, rosé) wine (white, red, rosé)

volaille poultry

Index

Acknowledgments

Marie-Pierre Moine's Acknowledgments

I am grateful to the many people who made this book happen. Dawn Henderson, Susan Downing, Caroline de Souza, and the in-house team at DK all excel at being nice to work with when the pressure is on. Jeni Wright and Norma MacMillan were guardian angels throughout. A huge thank you goes to Miranda Harvey, and to Jason Lowe. I also want to thank Valerie Berry, Christine Monteil at Château de Berne who first suggested Gui Gedda, Boulangerie Cassarini in Grasse, the Gedda family, Peter Usborne, and La Rivolte. And last but not least I pay tribute to Gui Gedda, a true Provençal and inspiring cook.

Publisher's Acknowledgments

Dorling Kindersley would like to thank Marie-Pierre Moine for her recipes and adaptations and her beautiful text throughout. Also thanks to Jeni Wright for initial concept development and flatplanning. And many thanks to Norma MacMillan and Miranda Harvey who managed the project skillfully and professionally.

Picture Credits

The publisher would like to thank the following for their kind permission to reproduce their photographs: (Key: a-above; b-below/bottom; c-centre; l-left; r-right; t-top)

Alamy Images: AA World Travel Library 273; Robert Fried 226; Peter Horree 248; Egmont Strigl / imagebroker 264-265; **Getty Images:** Klaus Hackenburg 267; Roy Rainford / Robert Harding 342-343; **Scope:** Christian Goupi 317

All other images © Dorling Kindersley
For further information see: www.dkimages.com